THE FIRST YEAR EXPERIENCE

THE FIRST YEAR EXPERIENCE

Start, stay and succeed at uni

Ann Game & Andrew Metcalfe

THE FEDERATION PRESS
2003

Published in Sydney by:
The Federation Press
PO Box 45, Annandale, NSW, 2038
71 John St, Leichhardt, NSW, 2040
Ph (02) 9552 2200 Fax (02) 9552 1681
E-mail: info@federationpress.com.au
Website: http://www.federationpress.com.au

National Library of Australia
Cataloguing-in-Publication entry

Game, Ann
The first year experience: start, stay, succeed at uni

ISNB 1 86287 470 0

1. Education, Higher 2. College students – Attitudes
3. Study skills. I. Metcalfe, Andrew W. II. Title

378

Typeset by The Federation Press, Leichhardt, NSW.
Printed by Ligare Pty Ltd, Riverwood, NSW.

Foreword

The two of us have a special interest in the experience of first year university students. Adrian Lee has taught at the University of New South Wales for more years than he will admit to and now has responsibility for ensuring that students have an interesting, challenging, relevant – and hopefully fun – learning experience as they work towards that final and sometimes seemingly far off graduation day. Craig McInnis, at the University of Melbourne, has conducted the major research studies in Australia on the transition of students from high school to university and strives to ensure that universities as a whole, and lecturers of first year students in particular, understand this transition and use this insight to provide support in what can be a stressful, yet rewarding, time.

The First Year Experience: Start, Stay and Succeed at Uni is written by authors who have a long and successful record of teaching first year students. Its key feature is that it also incorporates the views of students at a large and sometimes bewildering University. We hear of their hopes, their disappointments, their moments of enlightenment and above all some of the ways that they have found to enjoy both their university experience and academic success.

How to read, write and think may seem to be obvious skills, but the authors – building on their students' experiences – have provided some invaluable 'tips and traps' that if tried out, have the potential to not only improve performance, but make it more satisfying.

Students, as you commence one of the adventures of your life: that first year at uni, read this book. Reflect on whether the issues it covers are those that fit with your hopes of uni life. Dig deep and read these pages with some very specific goals. *Is there advice in here that I can actually use to change my behaviour so that not only will I get better marks at the end of year exams but also better enjoy the experience?* Sometimes you will have to be strict with yourself. For example, *keep a journal.* Is that really worth the effort?! Trust Ann Game and Andrew Metcalfe, they really know what works. Their students have told them.

Parents, friends and other supporters of first year students, read this book and also reflect: How can you use the advice and insights to support that student to not only succeed at university but also enjoy it. Strong support from home, particularly based on understanding of what the real issues of the first year experience are, is greatly valued by students (students sometimes have difficulty explaining what uni life is all about and how daunting it can be). If you yourself have not been to university, this book offers insights and ideas that can be positively used. If you are a graduate, reflect on whether the anecdotes ring true. Have things changed since your time? Are there more pressures? Are there different pressures? Dig deep and look for ways to support and not hinder your son, daughter, partner, nephew, niece or even grandchild.

As two academics and parents who know and love university life and the fulfilment it can bring to students – if we can provide the best environment and experience – we commend this small book to you and congratulate the authors. To us, one particular piece of advice (see page 72) is fundamental. *Enjoy your studies and you cannot fail.*

Professor Adrian Lee
Pro-Vice Chancellor (Education and Quality Improvement)
The University of New South Wales

Professor Craig McInnis
Director, Centre for the Study of Higher Education (CSHE)
The University of Melbourne

Contents

Acknowledgements

Our main thanks go to the students, tutors and mentors who have directly and indirectly contributed to the research for this book. In particular, we thank Amali Abeygunawardane, Tracy Ang, Melissa Anich, Adra Anthoney, Diana Borinski, Clare Burgett, Fiona Chia, Tess Connolly, Samantha Eddie, Jeffrey Fong, Felix Gentle, Meeray Ghaly, Peta Hinton, Guy Hungerford, Sophie Inwood, Jackie Kerr, Wing Shuen Lam, Dana Levin, Orna Marks, Sarah Mercer, Odette McWilliams, Stephanie Ng, Katie Rinaldi, Melissa Saxton, Stanya Sharota, Rebecca Stuart, Sarah Stone, Megan Taylor, Robyn Wheeler and Melanie Wong.

Research for this book was supported by a First Year Teaching Award organised by the office of the Pro-Vice Chancellor (Education) at the University of New South Wales. We also benefited from the Learning and Teaching Workshops organised by this office. In particular, we thank Adrian Lee, Michele Scoufis, Julie Grove, Sue Starfield and Stephanie Wilson.

We would also like to thank Rowland Hilder, Petri Calderon Larjanko, Rose Leontini, Yotam Weiner, Anita Sibrits, Jim Davidson and everyone at The Federation Press.

Throughout this book, we have quoted students' journals. These journals were written to capture the immediacy of ideas. They were not intended to be polished pieces of writing. We have changed students' names in the text.

INTRODUCTION

A student's story

A comment made by a first year student initiated this book. She complained that university had taken away the ingrained principles and processes of learning that had supported her at school, but that it hadn't replaced them.

This comment hardly came from the blue. As first year sociology lecturers and tutors, we've long been aware of this problem. But suddenly, with the help of this student, we saw what could be done about it.

In this book, we focus on the daily processes that constitute life at university, practices that support us through a lifetime of learning. The people who most enjoy the daily rhythms of university work do the most interesting and innovative work. And good marks follow good practices.

Because the book is practical, we have relied heavily on direct evidence of student experiences. Most conspicuously, you'll notice that the book is organised around quotations in which students directly describe the problems they face and discuss the helpful and unhelpful ways in which they've addressed these problems.

Here is the first of these. Written by Swee-Eng, a third year student, it is a description of the effect on her work of the sort of suggestions we make in this book.

I wrote an essay a few weeks ago, and it was one of the most difficult essay topics that I have ever encountered. When I started writing the essay, I felt really stuck, very insecure and unsure of what I was doing and thinking. Essentially I was 'deflated'. I did not want to do the essay and I had to take many breaks because I was so afraid of it that I just couldn't settle down and bring myself to approach it calmly. I spent countless hours trying to fish out what the essay question was expecting me to produce. Eventually, I just gave up writing for that day and went to bed.

I think my block was caused by my over-eagerness and anxiousness to get it done. I was very concerned about the grade I would get, because I needed to maintain a distinction average in order to be eligible for Honours. I wanted to do really well also because this is my last semester here at UNSW so I just wanted to see what I was capable of producing.

But eventually I realised that sitting at my desk and trying to write in that panicked state of mind was a total waste of time, and I knew that trying forcibly to unblock the block would never work. It was then that I gave up trying – trying too hard to make things work! I resigned to my fate (in this case that painful block) and began looking through the list of potential references for the essay and choosing those that were the most enjoyable for me instead of the essays that were really difficult (but very 'intellectual' in the academic sense). And that was when things started to change.

One of the things on the reading list was a story. I loved it so much that I just had to include it in my essay.

By doing so I began to enjoy my essay more and more and I totally forgot about whether I sounded 'academic' enough. I kept it simple and really related to it! This essay was different from all the others because I put a part of myself in it. I began to feel that this was a really good essay, but then as I progressed to another point I began to feel detached from the essay again and I started to question my choice in using the story's analogy. Then I referred back to the essay question again and felt even more confused by it. I wasn't very sure that I was doing what was required of me. This led on to my second major block in writing this particular essay!

Then I thought about the advice about letting go of self-consciousness and trusting my instincts, so I decided to stop doubting myself and give myself a chance to explore what was being brought up, and I tried to express myself as simply as I could. By doing so, letting go of the pressure and embracing my thought with humility, trust and love, I started to rewrite my essay. I approached it in a non-committed way, unsure of whether I would sound silly or be overly simplistic in my explanations. And before I knew it, it was all over. I embraced the insecurity and it enabled me to let my thoughts and writing flow.

By the time I had to submit it, it surprised me that I was not expecting a good grade. I mean of course I was a little anxious about whether I got it right! But it did not overwhelm me as it usually does! My lecturer returned the essays to us on Monday and I was fully prepared to receive a Credit for the effort I put in. But what really shocked me was the grade of High Distinction. This is the first time I've been awarded this grade! It really boggled my mind! (heeheehee) I'm just upset that I did not learn all this sooner, because it would have made writing up essays and reports less of a chore and more of an experience to cherish, regardless of the results and consequences. (Swee-Eng)

It is impossible to read such accounts without feeling inspired. *This* is what university is about. *This* is its potential to improve people's lives. When Swee-Eng tried to protect her grade-average by giving an examiner what she imagined they wanted, she felt inadequate and exhausted. The work drained her. But when she courageously 'got into it', following her arguments wherever they led, she learned a lot more – about the course and about her own capacities and ideas. She felt she was given energy, and a richer and more interesting life. And isn't it funny that the work that she did for its own sake led to better grades.

Swee-Eng's laugh is the delighted recognition that the most important things in university life simply and easily fall into place if we are open and honest in our relations with the work. This is the lesson we want this book to offer.

What matters most at university

Fifty academics are gathered for a workshop on 'best teaching practice'. There are psychologists, economists, lawyers, microbiologists, physicists, architects, historians, accountants, food technologists, sociologists, art theorists, designers, information technologists, literary critics, librarians. Because most have never met before, and know little of each other's fields of expertise, there is an anxiety in the room. We're worried that we may have nothing worthwhile to say to colleagues from such disparate disciplines.

Then the workshop convenor asks us to identify our main teaching goal. This question is so simple that it disarms all the sophisticated statements we'd planned to make. When we begin going around the room, no one mentions their own specialist fields. Instead we find that we're all speaking the same language.

We all want students to become creative thinkers who know how to analyse problems and evaluate arguments, how to locate whatever information they need, and how to develop and present original arguments in a variety of modes.

We want students who can organise their work effectively and work collaboratively.

We want students to learn an open attitude to the development of knowledge.

If our graduates thought that we'd taught them everything they needed to know, we'd have failed: we want students who are prepared for a lifetime of retraining and rethinking, for a lifetime of learning.

Although university disciplines expect students to master conspicuously different sets of knowledge, the knowledge of a subject matter is only a stepping stone, a necessary part of the process that teaches us what new things we need to learn: what different arguments, what better theories and what more useful applications are possible. This is why the content of university courses is neither fixed nor the comprehensive treatment of a subject matter.

When university examinations question students about curriculum content, the examiners' real interest is in what the students' answers reveal about their ways of working. Examiners want to know, for example, if students have learned how to identify key issues and concentrate on problems. Do students read in ways appropriate to university? How creative are their relations with the material they're studying? How do they deal with competing viewpoints? Are there signs of depth in their thinking? Is their work well organised and are their arguments well presented?

Although university disciplines differ in subject matter, all teach the deeper discipline of openness to learning. This is what matters most at university.

ARRIVING

Expectations

What I wanted to get from university was a kind of legitimacy with which to establish my own uniqueness and specialness. I was willing to submit to the dreary economics classes (they weren't all dreary) because I thought knowing that stuff, understanding it their way, would give me a kind of legitimacy when I attacked the economic way of thinking. Me. The plan of attack was a plan for me, not a plan for ... I don't know how to put it. A plan for the world? I didn't have imaginative reveries in which world economic problems were solved by my insight, but I did have imaginative reveries where my writing about said problems earned me plaudits.

Thinking of this I have a picture of the poor terrified students who make their way into university, so proud of their Tertiary Entrance Rankings but at the same time so terrified of the adult world they are now entering, unsure of how they will make their way in it, wanting to be hugely successful (because modest and realistic success couldn't be enough, not in a big place like this!) and dreading the failure to achieve it. Idealism very rapidly turns into cynicism, yet these two aren't so different in their composition. Both are a defence against the simple and present world which holds out only exactly what is there. (Luke)

We all know that expectations can be a problem. Think of your travel experiences. However wonderful your destination turns out to be, it can never exactly match the postcard or travel book. As long as you're searching for these preconceptions, you'll be unable to experience the place as it is.

Expectations can likewise be a problem for students arriving at university. You cannot do without expectations, but, if you're unable to suspend these expectations, you won't be able to see university with fresh eyes. What you'll see is a series of confirmations and disappointments that distract you from what you're actually experiencing.

Look at Luke's case. Had he held onto his preconceptions, he'd have been disappointed. By suspending them, he let university teach him that its role is to *change* understandings and expectations. What you get from university will always be something that you couldn't have expected when you began.

But it is a strange and wonderful process. When Luke stopped looking for his uniqueness, he discovered that what he wanted was there all along. He is now creatively fulfilled by the daily work process of university life. Everyday he is surprised by what he can produce. When Luke stopped pursuing his expectation, he found it unexpectedly met.

This is Luke's case, but it will be the same with yours.

Hold your expectations lightly and don't let them interfere with your openness to the world around you. If you get involved in university life for its own sake, you will find that exciting and satisfying things happen to you. They won't be what you expected, but later you will suddenly realise: *this* was what you wanted all along.

Suspend your expectations when you arrive at university and surprising things will happen.

Life in the big city

> *Adulthood seems to be an exclusive club when you're a child. A time when I felt like an adult was when I moved to Sydney to go to university. I felt like I was independent, able to make my own decisions. (Vicky)*

Many students arrive at university in a post-exam euphoria. Their good results in their high school finals have won them entry into the adult world of university. Childhood is over and the rest of life is beginning. It's an exciting and proud day in the life story of every student, and, as Luke suggests, students are expecting to be welcomed with congratulations.

What is it that students actually meet on their first days? The first thing you'll probably notice is the size of university. To give some sense of this scale, here are some statistics relating to our own university. Since it was established about 50 years ago, it has given out about 175,000 degrees. Presently, it has 35,000 students in any year. Over 8000 of these are overseas students, who between them represent 90 nationalities. About 22,000 students are enrolled in bachelor's degree courses and almost 2000 are studying for doctorates. There are the equivalent of 2000 full-time academic staff and 2600 non-academic staff. There are nine faculties, 75 schools, 78 research centres, three institutes, five field stations, six teaching hospitals and eight residential colleges. There are 400 different undergraduate and postgraduate programs available. The main campus occupies 38 hectares and the university has 85 permanent buildings. The university library has over 2 million items. The university's total assets are valued at $1.42 billion, and its total income in any year exceeds $500 million.

Even if you attend a university half this size, you're still participating in a very large institution, and this fact alone will influence your relationships and experiences. Here are some of the dynamics we would expect.

Meeting only a relatively small number of their colleagues, people at university may develop personal identifications at the class or school level but the links at the faculty and university level will tend to be emotionally weak and bureaucratic. There will be elaborate rules to ensure accountability and efficiency across the university, and these rules will strictly standardise the way enrolments and assessments are organised. Staff numbers, student numbers, passwords and identity cards with passport photographs will be required for access to any point in this bureaucratic system.

The campus will be so large that few people can find their way around it without a grid-referenced map. People will tend to remain in their own districts, but when they have to move through public spaces they will often feel alone, or alone in a crowd of strangers headed in unknown directions. Coordination of activities across the large campus will require a strict regime of clocks and timetables and room bookings, reducing the flexibility possible in classroom relations.

It will help you deal with university procedures if you appreciate their scale.

First day

The first day at university sees a disparity between the personal focus of students and the institutional logics of university enrolment procedures. Instead of a welcome, there are snaking queues that turn each student into *another* student. Before they've even enrolled, students are feeling disillusioned.

> *On enrolment day we were all herded through the process with a student number and not so much as a smile. It was understandable as they had a lot to get through but all the same it left me feeling very intimidated and anonymous. I think it hit me especially hard seeing as at school I was known by a lot of students, being a school captain. (Belinda)*

> *I collided head on with the Big Wide World. School had been the Age of Innocence. My idealisation of university as being the amazing years of my life faded into an abyss of obscurity. With a student number pinned to my forehead, I felt devalued and unimportant, one among many, another face in the crowd. (Jessica)*

> *I don't know what I expected, but it is quite a shock to come straight out of school, where everyone knows you and talks to you, and go into an environment where no one knows you and you are seen as a number. At enrolment I entered quite excited at what I thought was going to be an easy and friendly way into university. I was quite taken aback by the gruff and uncaring reply. I joined the queue already feeling disheartened. (Jae)*

Students expect university to acknowledge their school achievements and their new independence. Instead enrolment day can leave them feeling like another unimportant face in the crowd.

Be patient during your first days at university. Everyone is having a trying time.

Shutting down

We commonly deal with feelings of disappointment by closing off from those who've hurt us. Christine provides a good description of the defensive cycle involved:

> *A seemingly minor error with my subject allocation led to a nightmarish process. Enrolment day was busy and rigidly structured with many lines and rather harassed looking staff. I feel quite intimidated by some, as they were rather abrupt and impatient with questions and queues. Though they were not exactly rude, by looking almost through me I felt less than what I was. I can now in hindsight appreciate the enormous task that lay ahead of the staff that day with thousands of students to deal with, but at that time I felt very disillusioned.*

By being treated as just another number, you felt that you were not important enough to be concerned with. People looked almost through you, without really seeing a person before them. You felt like they weren't really listening to what you were saying and they didn't really care either way. As the day progressed I started to become more and more sensitive, almost shutting down. I became defensive when they asked questions, as I felt they were implying the mistake lay with me when it was an error made by administration. I felt myself tightening up both physically and emotionally. My hands and jaws clenched and my mind refused to see any thing before me.

I felt as if I was a problem, to be handed over to one person after another to be solved. I then stopped responding to the people around me. I did to them what I felt they were doing to me. I didn't want to be regarded as just another number.

I was frustrated with the process, I was angry and upset so I shut myself off from it, so that it couldn't touch me. It was almost like I was separating myself from it, so that it could not affect me. It is almost a never ending cycle because everyone is objectifying those around them from the fear of being objectified themselves. So, I suppose the question to ask is why we fear so much? What makes us want to do to others what we ourselves do not want? Is there a way to break this cycle? (Christine)

As Christine observes, feelings of hurt are worsened by the common defences used against them. The alternative is to stay open. The first and major step toward this openness is to acknowledge how you yourself are feeling. Admit that you feel hurt, and you won't then be divided against yourself, feeling one way but acting as if you felt another.

Christine offers another valuable suggestion when she notes that 'it is almost a never ending cycle because everyone is objectifying those around them from the fear of being objectified themselves'. This recognition is another step towards connecting with those whom you've been denying. If they too are defending themselves, you and they must feel something in common, and, if you suspend the temptation to find someone or something to blame, this common ground will be a basis for compassion. Once you can notice the vulnerability of others – other students in the queue, the harried clerical workers – your compassion will bring a sense of belonging.

Things become easier if you stay open. Lucy tells us how this works:

> *The funny thing is that when someone connects with you and stops looking at you like a problem or object, the problem you have is shared with the person and figuring it out becomes easy and things just come to you. So you can change the relation to the problem. (Lucy)*

Openness and compassion are the only protection against the feelings of hurt and disappointment.

Taking it easy

Universities are big cities: impersonality and fragmentation are part of their nature, even though they also produce niches of intimacy. You don't expect personal recognition when you walk in a big city, and for that reason you don't blame yourself or the city when it doesn't occur. You learn instead to appreciate the city on its own terms and to find ways to enjoy being part of its hum. It is the same with university.

Given this size and complexity, it isn't only the overseas students who feel they've arrived in a foreign country when they start university. You will have to familiarise yourself with a huge amount of information before you even get to choose your courses, and it is offered in the bureaucratic jargon of UOCs, HPWs, GPAs, prerequisites, exemptions and major sequences.

It's easy to feel demoralised and frustrated by this process. Once you acknowledge the size of the institution, however, you realise that initial confusions are unavoidable. All universities could improve their bureaucratic procedures, but a degree of disorientation is a necessary part of learning your way around a place this big. With 35,000 students selecting courses from the 400 different programs, it is sometimes amazing that university works as well as it does.

So give yourself time to get used to university. Take it easy. Ask for help. Remember that you're not *supposed* to know everything. No one does, not even the lecturers and administrators.

And don't be too proud or too shy to do the library tours, orientation week activities and peer mentoring programs available early in your first year. By highlighting your status as a newcomer, these activities may make you feel awkward and self-conscious, but no one will notice or think less of you. The very impersonality of universities precludes such judgments.

If you know anything about university, you know that everyone needs help finding their way about.

Unique and special

Maybe I should cherish the uni life and stop treating everyone as an object. Because when these years are over, I won't be able to come back here. I will have no chance to see the good view from the library lawn because I may be working in Hong Kong in the future. Also I won't have the chance to walk the crowded university walk, since I will be working in an office located in Central. If I keep treating other students as objects, I will have an objectified memory in the future. I really don't want to have such 'cold' memory. (Jasmin)

Jasmin notes the difference it makes when you cherish your experience, savouring the view from the library lawn and the bustle of the student crowds. What an amazing place university is. What a buzz to be here! Now!

What's more, you *belong* here. Although university can seem aloof, it is also a wayfarer's inn that finds a special place for countless thousands of passing students, whatever their shape and size, whatever their special interests, whatever fate has in store for them. No one is an interloper because no one owns a university, not the lecturers, not the students, not the administrative staff, not the Vice-Chancellor, not the government.

As a place of meeting, university reaches a long way. On your graduation day you'll be able to reserve seats in the auditorium specifically for your grandparents, and when the Dean and Vice-Chancellor welcome the relatives of the graduates, you'll hear the genuine warmth in their voices. University is too large to be personal, but it is this impersonality that allows it to welcome so many people.

Once you've been accepted for enrolment, you need prove nothing else: you are a part of university. What your university wants is for you to find your own way of contributing to its ongoing life. Lecturers and other students are eager for your involvement and interest. If you set aside the noise and distraction of the rushing around, you'll find that university life is sustained by a hum of creativity.

Once you're enrolled, you belong at university. You don't need to keep proving yourself.

INTEREST

Being interested

Students want university to be interesting, but what generates interest? What happens to us when we gain or lose interest? How can we make university life more interesting? Here is a student story that can tell us a lot about interest. Tian is explaining what happened when he encountered the unfamiliar language of the philosopher Martin Buber:

> *To begin with, Buber's piece was boring and confusing, his language was from another planet for all I cared. I read the whole piece and managed to vaguely understand a few lines. It was overall a frustrating experience. Later on, during a trip to uni, finding myself bored out of my mind, I looked in my bag to find that the course reader was the only thing I could read. Because I had been told that Buber's article may be helpful to my essay, I began reading. Again I could not really understand what it was about but this time there was no irritation on my part. I wasn't reading with the aim of the essay in my mind but just reading. As I progressed not much changed except my attitude to it, but now there were lines that really got me. From there on things started to fall into place, and I finally understood what Buber had been talking about. It interested me and I actually read it a few more times not*

> *only because I had to anyway for this essay but because I wanted to. In retrospect, I think the problem the first time I read it was my approach. I was sceptical, forcing myself to try to understand, but at the same time unwilling to open myself to learn. (Tian)*

Tian couldn't find the meaning by forcefully seeking it. When he treated reading as a test of his own competence, the words scared him, and he was forced to defend himself by setting up barriers. The words were 'confusing', 'vague', 'boring', 'frustrating', 'from another planet'. But later, on the bus, instead of trying to *get* the words, he read in a relaxed way, with curiosity. This attitude gave the words the chance to get *him*, and him the chance to get *them*.

Tian uses a good expression to describe his changed relation to the reading: it came to interest him. Interest is a word we often use casually, but its etymology reminds us of its significance. *Inter* means 'between' and *esse* means 'to be'. Interest is life between. The interest that allows creative work at university doesn't come just from the student, nor just from the object studied, but from their relationship. Tian's open attitude made a difference to that relationship.

When students are involved in their studies they lose their self-consciousness, but they find that in learning about the world they also learn about themselves. As new ideas fall into place, the journey of education is both outward and inward. When we know deeply, it is not because we know a lot, but because we know and live with this sense of interest.

If your attitude is open, interest will emerge.

Enthusiasm

To begin with, Tian had to 'force himself' to read Buber, but reading was easy on the bus: 'I actually read it a few more times not only because I had to anyway for this essay but because I wanted to'. The energy and direction that Tian needed became available as soon as he 'opened himself to learn'.

Here is another example of energy and direction coming from interest. Rachel is trying to understand her generally soulless high school career by thinking about the exceptional experience:

> *My school had a reputation to keep up, and so it emphasised the importance of the HSC mark from the word go. As a result, my education, up until now, has largely consisted of going through the motions. My heart was rarely involved, but I had to complete it because if I didn't my HSC marks would be doomed, thus reducing my chances of getting into uni. I think this lack of heart is where this 'last-minute' way of doing assignments developed from.*
>
> *During year 12, there was one exception to this attitude. Earth and Environmental Science was my absolute favourite subject. I was fascinated by it. One of the assignments we were given involved us all having to*

trace a species back to another species and comment on the pattern of evolution. I was given the Petrolacosaurus and had to see how it's related to modern-day crocodiles.

Resources on the net were limited, even more scarce in library books. I did manage to find, however, the personal website of a rather interesting guy dressed up in some bizarre tribal head piece who had a PhD in the evolution of crocodiles!

Initially we corresponded by email but I had so many questions that we both decided it would be easier to meet up over coffee somewhere. 'Dr Croc,' as his personalised number plate said, rocked up to the café on his motorbike, and we instantly clicked. He was the coolest guy I'd ever seen! Loud and crazy and bursting with a wealth of knowledge that he was so keen on sharing with me. I'm not sure how long we talked for, but he taught me all I needed to know and more. I was fascinated right from the start.

The most important part was I was inspired. He hadn't just given me the information I needed to pass my assignment, but the desire to learn, the desire to find out more and more about it. I put more effort into that assignment than ever because I had lost track of the marks involved. I ended up getting full marks for the assignment, but that didn't matter to me. I had learnt about an amazing evolutionary process and had met one of the most amazing people I've ever seen in the process. No way was that a 'last-minute' effort. I loved what I was doing and that made all the difference.

Relating this back to other situations, I think the only reason students put themselves under the pressure of the

> *last minute is because they really don't want to be doing them. They are disengaged or disinterested. Watching TV, eating a snack ... anything would be more interesting than doing the essay. If students were truly engaged in their work, like I was with my crocodile assessment, then the sheer act of learning is a stronger motivation than any. However, if students aren't interested in it, then they need the motivation and pressure they put themselves under in order to get it done. (Rachel)*

There are some important lessons here. The first is that you need not rely on determination or a rush of adrenalin to energise your work. Enthusiasm is a livelier, more creative and focused alternative. Second, it's not up to you to generate enthusiasm since it is simply a manifestation of interest. Enthusiasm is always there if you love what you're doing. Third, enthusiasm is celebratory rather than reward-seeking, requiring neither internal goals nor external pressures.

Interest will give you the enthusiasm you need.

Lacking enthusiasm

> *I guess being bored is often a defence mechanism, as well as being the fear of losing control or seeming uncool. I also experience the fear of not really understanding the lecture, and rather than ask for assistance, it is much*

simpler to label the class as boring and forget about it. Boredom is a cover for our feelings of insecurity. (Rossella)

I don't really have anything to write about. I feel blank inside, nothing takes me, and it makes me feel a bit worthless, useless. Nothing to say. What's the point of sharing your writing with someone when you have nothing worthwhile to say? They may as well be staring at a blank piece of paper, for all the good it does. Shameful and stupid. I feel like a blanket's drawn over my body, so that I can't feel anything. (Erin)

Without enthusiasm and interest, university work is a trial. One response to this, Rossella's, is to blame someone or something else (the reading, the course, the lecture). Another response, Erin's, is to blame yourself.

It is important to realise that these undesirable responses are normal and nothing in themselves to be afraid or ashamed of. Don't blame yourself for blaming. If you set up enthusiasm as a perfection to be attained, you'll only raise fears about your adequacy.

So, if we cannot force interest into our studies, what *are* we to do about unenthusiastic responses? The answer is beautifully simple. We allow ourselves to become interested in these responses themselves. Rather than seeking to overcome them, we learn from them.

Here is a simple example to show how this works. Tian spoke of protecting himself with scepticism and Rossella spoke of not wanting to seem 'uncool'. These are very common attitudes at university. *What's this got to do with the real world? Can't we have something more up to date? Who cares about all this stuff anyway? Do you expect me to believe this? Why don't they tell me something I don't already know?* While scepticism can be constructive, in these cases it stands in the way of honest engagement with readings and lectures, and therefore stands in the way of interest.

The rhetorical nature of these questions indicates that there is something that students don't want to face. But if you notice your blasé scepticism, and stay with it, you can learn what it's afraid of. You'll be led to answering your own questions: what *do* they expect? what *has* this got to do with the world?

In Rossella's case, reflections on her lack of enthusiasm led her to acknowledge her deeper fears and concerns, and this brought alive again her sense of being implicated in the situation. She realised that the attitude she brought to the lecture shaped the experience of it.

When the situation is faced directly, you'll have a better chance to explore it calmly, less personally, with more discrimination. What *are* the reasons for the course being structured as it is? What effect *would* it have on your life if you took these ideas seriously? What's the best thing to do if the lecturer *is* out of date?

By becoming interested in the blasé attitude itself, you've become interested in the world again. You've found a fresh source of energy for university.

Stay with the negative feelings and they will lead you back to interest and enthusiasm.

PROCRASTINATION

Procrastination and pressure

Students enjoy telling rueful stories that identify procrastination as their major writing problem. Although details vary, the stories all present students who know they're acting foolishly but have no real desire to change.

When they're about to begin work, these students realise that the carpet needs vacuuming and the dog needs a walk. By the time all the chores are done, it's too late to start that day, or they're no longer in the mood. So, tomorrow! They will *definitely* start tomorrow. Inevitably, procrastinating students write all their term's essays in the final week, vowing, vainly, never again to allow procrastination to get them into such a mess. Here is how two students, Sunnie and Christine, discuss their problems:

> *Procrastination is definitely my middle name. Even a psychic once told my mother that I was a great procrastinator, lazy, who could do anything I wanted if only I'd start. Yes, that's pretty much me in a nutshell. Once I'm at my desk, I'm fine. Once I get started, there's usually no stopping me. It's a matter of getting my bottom on that seat. Instead the carpet suddenly needs vacuuming. During exam time, my room is always spotless but in every other month of the year, it's the usual bomb. I really admire – and envy – those people who can plan an essay and use all the available time*

constructively. But that's just not me. I perform best under pressure (maybe not best, but to date, adequately).

I've also come to realise that there is a safety net in the night-before technique. If you finish the night before, and receive an almost expected though not hoped for bad mark, you get over it quickly because you know you didn't pay the deserved attention. Whereas if you actually worked your butt off and did draft after draft and perfected it (or so you thought) and still received a non-favourable mark, you are absolutely shattered. Procrastination is a fool-proof non-disappointment mechanism. It's a bad frame of mind to live by, but 75% of students, including me, swear by it. (Sunnie)

When given an assignment, I start early with all good intentions, but I waste time, I put off doing it. Even as I'm doing this I tell myself that I am going to regret all the procrastination in a few weeks time, but I still do it. I'm not exactly sure why. It is almost like I enjoy the pressure, the clarity that occurs in my mind when under immense pressure, when you know you cannot put anything off for any longer, so you just do it. You have to ignore or just tackle the uncomfortable feelings you have. OK, so it could be the fact that I am not comfortable or relaxed about what I have to do, which makes me put it off until I can no longer ignore it. I can't sit with my work, so I avoid it. There is something about it which I cannot control.

I find that my desire for neatness and order is particularly acute when I am stressed, sleep-deprived and overworked – so pretty much when I have a lot of exams and assignments due in. I don't like dealing with new work, I find it overwhelming. When I am not on top of my work, the sight of a messy unorganised room makes me feel frustrated and angry. I stop whatever I am doing to clean and reorganise.

The start is always the most difficult, as you feel as if you are diving into the middle of the ocean. You feel embarrassed and scared by what you have written. It is never good enough, it just doesn't sound right. Putting words on paper is sometimes like putting yourself on paper and that can be a little intimidating at times. (Christine)

Hearing the uncertain tone with which students discuss their laziness, and noticing that Sunnie and Christine actually insist on their preference for pressure, we've come to suspect that procrastination isn't simply a failure of will or time-management. It isn't primarily an issue of reluctance, laziness, carelessness, indifference or disorganisation, as the stories suggest. These cool reasons are alibis for more intense processes of fear and shame.

The pressure of the deadline is the unacknowledged purpose and not the unintended consequence of procrastination. Despite complaining about deadlines, many of us illicitly depend on pressure.

Be honest about the reasons for procrastination.

Writer's block

To understand this addiction to crisis, we must appreciate the fears that underlie Sunnie's and Christine's descriptions.

The most celebrated writers, who produce the most graceful prose, suffer similar problems to students writing essays. As writers, there will be days when we are blocked, when we lose hope, when the words are sullen. These are normal experiences. Often, though, we don't realise this. We're convinced that we are alone in our experience, that the problems have only arisen because of our own inadequacies.

To help break the conspiracy of silence, here are accounts of the ordinary experience of two students who are particularly accomplished writers:

> *As I diligently sat at my desk evening after evening I was gradually realising that I did not know anything. My years at university were surely wasted, for I certainly lacked the sort of total knowledge that this assessment had presumed of me. Feeling empty in this hungry condition, I thought that I could know enough for the assignment only if I read more. And so I began what could only be described as a ravaging of books, journal articles and Internet sites. As I read more and more, the futility of my quest for satiety became apparent: there was always more to read.*
>
> *A few days into my binge, I began to feel bloated. I was full of names and ideas and yet the mass sat in me, undigested, crowded, their relationships unresolved. There were so many ideas that they now all appeared the same to me. I became 'blocked' in a very physical sense, feeling as though, right in the centre of the chest, somewhere above the solar plexus, there was something compacting into a single point of ever increasing density.*
>
> *Had I finally reached the fullness I had yearned for? Was I finally ready to sit down and pour my knowledge onto the page? I was surely full, but I could not write, for my fullness was stuffiness, a heavy burden. I was full of names and ideas and yet I was empty of knowledge: I could not write anything; I had not yet learnt anything. Things became so bad that I could not bear to look at any printed material, not even at a book of paintings, because I feared that it might generate more ideas. (Katherine)*

I don't feel 'blocked' – I'm not even there yet. I feel reluctant, overwhelmed and very scared of my essay(s). I am self-conscious and my hand hurts and I have an itchy leg and everything seems more important and less important at the same time. I am frustrated and even annoyed by how messy my writing is and how presumptuous I was to assume that I could write this essay. I have that 'I have no knowledge' feeling, but instead of wanting to read I want to walk away.

I am angry with my work because what seemed to be a flash of inspiration, brilliance, stand alone good writing, in between pages of crap, turns out to be quite the contrary. I let someone else read it and they comment on my 'crap' and ignore my 'brilliance'.

I've thought about changing to another topic, but it's too easy, it's like defeat, and so I have to turn slowly back to my essay, ashamed and petrified of the confrontation that lies in actually seeing the face of my essay as it is. I am also so angry that I have this stupid mental block that won't let me write. I want to write straight away like my teachers. I hate the process. I want to be brilliant. (Camilla)

All writers experience blocks. What makes a difference is how you respond.

Blocks are not a dead-end but an integral part of the writing process.

Staying with the mess

> *I've thought about changing to another topic, but it's too easy, it's like defeat, and so I have to turn slowly back to my essay, ashamed and petrified of the confrontation that lies in actually seeing the face of my essay as it is. (Camilla)*

Camilla has reason to be grateful for the process that taught her how to write this essay. It was when she felt the impulse to flee that she knew she had to stay and face the issue that scared her. And through this process of sitting-with, she came to imagine the words and arguments that weren't available to her when she was fantasising a one-draft brilliance. The marker of Camilla's essay told us that he wished he could write as well. He gave it 92 per cent.

The openness to inspiration that Camilla experienced is not some fantastically easy path to success. It is itself a form of discipline, involving the courage to sit with the unfinished work and hear what it calls for. Through this process of being interested, things that you couldn't have previously imagined will happen.

Whereas procrastinating students fantasise that teachers and 'really good' students write from a position of security, that their success derives from having learned all there is to know, including how to write cleanly, a bemused and humble attitude is more characteristic of students who get high marks.

> *When people have congratulated me on my results, I always feel slightly embarrassed as there are two questions in my mind. 1) Where do these thoughts*

> *come from? 2) Is this force mine? The process is utterly mysterious. It is a kind of reaction that I simply expect or wait to happen, but I do not own or control this creative impulse. It happens to me. I am merely its recipient, its agent. Sometimes I wonder whether these thoughts are even mine. Hence the ancient Greek muses? (Lilly)*

The mysterious process that Lilly describes isn't ethereal. It is a discipline that allows new ideas to come from the mess of the ordinary and everyday.

If you stay with the mess of the process, an interesting essay will unfold.

Rushing through

Imagine this situation. It's the night before an unwritten essay is due, and you're feeling overwhelmed. And then, miraculously, the increasing pressure of the deadline triggers an adrenalin rush: action replaces anxiety, self-consciousness gives way to the speed that Christine describes as clarity, and the next thing you know the essay is written. You slide it into the collection-box next morning, saved from disaster.

The procrastination-and-pressure approach to essay writing attempts to avoid the actual process of writing –

the listening, letting go, sitting with and waiting, the notes, lists, drafts and redrafts. The rush allows students to move from being the student with an essay due to the student with the essay done, without having to attend to the uncertain and adventurous condition in-between.

To appreciate the consequences of this avoidance, think of the tourists who rush through foreign countries, eager to *do* the country, without actually taking the risk of *being in* the strangeness. Whether you're the tourist or the last-minute essay writer, this rushing method means that you emerge unchanged from the experience, that you learn nothing on the way.

Many university students 'swear by' this pressure-based method because they've never experienced better ways of avoiding the paralysis of self-consciousness. So, before we discuss these alternatives in the next chapter, let us be clear about the drawbacks of procrastination-and-pressure.

- Little or nothing is learned from the actual writing of these essays. Alternative arguments and new ideas must be either set aside or quickly accommodated within an established schema, for fear they will obstruct your progress.
- The rushed method becomes completely unviable when longer projects are required.
- These essays are worse than those written through a more considered process.
- Pressure is a way of work and life that perpetuates the fear it seeks to flee.

- This way of working denies the possibility of experiencing the joy of writing.
- You're not giving yourself the chance to learn the skills and disciplines of thinking and writing that people need in their professional lives.

The procrastination-and-pressure writing method precludes the possibility of learning.

WRITING

There are two important suggestions in this chapter. One is that good writing relies on a complex relation between goal-orientation and playfulness. The other is that good writing is built up through different stages, each requiring different skills. The layering of this drafting process enriches an essay and makes writing one of the most exciting experiences of university life. If writing isn't serious fun, there is something seriously wrong with your relation to it.

Writing, reading and thinking are intertwined, so you'll find writing suggestions in other chapters too. Our focus here is on the most practical issues.

Getting started

This is Anna, reflecting on the process of starting an essay:

> *I didn't know where to start or what to do – I didn't know the right word or right process. So my intro was simply – 'How do I start? Where do I start?' And then 'I think I'm just going to write and let my pen take me wherever it goes as thinking too much and trying too hard really seems to get me nowhere.' So I just started writing and writing, and when I stopped and counted I had written seven pages without really realising. It's just good when that happens. Like I was able to get into it even though I had no idea how to start.*

> Starting. *That's the biggest issue. You think too much. You want the essay to be perfect. But in the process your flow and natural grace are inhibited. On realising that starting was my problem I guess I decided not to formally start. So I didn't and it got me somewhere. Then afterwards, when I guess I'd basically finished the body of my essay, I was able to come back and scrap the entire first part. Not because it was useless – it was essential in leading me into the right frame of mind. (Anna)*

Students with writer's block fear it is too hard to start an essay while those who write fluently *know* it is too hard. Good writers do not start their essays. We mean this in two senses. First, the question of where to begin the essay is suspended because the right place to start is *anywhere*. Second, most of Anna's time was spent *just writing*, not writing *an essay*. The project could not stay foremost in her mind if the writing was to stay lively and instructive.

In the end, good essays fall into place. They are not written so much as compiled, edited and re-edited from the writing that has emerged.

Do not start essays.
Do not write essays.

Journals

Whatever course you're doing, whatever creative pursuit you follow in life, we recommend you maintain a journal. A journal keeps you involved in your studies, learning what it is that you know or need to learn. An academic journal also lets you write your essays before you know you're doing it.

A journal doesn't ask you to be clever. All it asks is that you regularly set aside time for honest writing that relates, in whatever obscure way, to your courses. If you serve your journal, it will serve you, doing the key essay-producing work while you're occupied with this more immediate task. It will allow you to think and write more courageously than you could have yourself. Rosemary put it this way:

> *I have always wanted to be a writer but have avoided actually writing anything for fear of failure. In writing the journal last year I wrote many personal thoughts and reflections without confining myself to what I considered would be valid to the course specifically. It was probably the first time I'd written something I could reflect on later and consider what was actually going on in my head and how these thoughts were born. Essentially it was the start of an honest relationship with myself through my writing. (Rosemary)*

When Rosemary speaks of 'an honest relationship with myself through my writing', she identifies the key to a university journal.

Here are some suggestions for the use of a journal.

- *Let go.* You mustn't worry about being correct and proper. Have fun, follow your curiosity, work through questions that matter to you. A journal is not, however, a 'dear diary' of self-disclosure: it is about possibilities that don't need to be turned into self-definitions.
- *Don't insist that the writing always be useful or relevant.* If ideas seem interesting, that is reason enough for writing. You cannot know in advance where the insights lie and you will always learn something through the process itself.
- *Write short.* Use diagrams to develop your sense of associations. Use short notes to record your flashes of clarity, for unrecorded flashes fade from memory or seem too insubstantial to be taken seriously. Make free-association lists of every point that occurs to you in relation to any topic or idea.
- *Write long.* Lists and notes aren't substitutes for writing long. Because the journal is a space for thinking through writing, trains of thought must not be prejudged or cut short. Spell out issues in the simplest possible language, remembering that sophisticated code words are ways of avoiding potential issues. Draw out implications as far as you can, trying out the ideas in different domains. By writing long you will also generate material to work with at a later stage.
- *Write as you read*, about both the content of your readings and your responses to them. You'll learn how the content and form of your readings interrelate and how your pre-cognitive responses can teach you about the ideas 'in' the text.

- *Be honest* in your responses to texts, lectures, tutorials. Writing about feelings allows you to learn from them.
- *Treat your journal as a course reading.* Read your journal with the same curiosity as other course readings, and use it as a prompt for more writing, a secondary analysis at a deeper level. Are there issues you can spell out more? Are there key words that you notice? Can you draw out the assumptions on which your habits of thought rely? Are there tensions between what you wrote in one place and another? Look at the items on your lists with curiosity and see if you can find another level of associations based on the metaphorics of the words. Use an etymological dictionary to unearth the associations between words.
- *Read softly.* Read your journal without harsh judgment. There is always life in unguarded writing, but you may need to be gentle to feel it.
- *Do not tidy up.* By handwriting in an exercise book you may avoid the temptation, offered by a keyboard's delete button, to make things neat and tidy. As a record of a work process, a journal will help you learn from the mess necessary for all creative activity.
- *Write regularly.* It is good practice to set a regular time for writing in your journal, perhaps first thing in the morning or last thing at night, perhaps before and/or after your lecture.
- *Allow the journal to guide your essays.* Reread your journal as you work on any assignment. It will help you recall what most interests you. You can probably also use

journal entries in your first draft (but remember to reconsider this material as the essay develops).

- *The journal is for you.* So find a form, rhythm and way of being with it that works for you as a learning support. If it feels like duty, it's not working.

All writers need journals.

First drafts

A first draft is no more than an extended journal entry. It is qualitatively different from subsequent drafts because it involves the generation of a text with which to work.

A first draft is written in an open and unpressured condition. As well as the reassurance of knowing that no one else need read it, there is the comfort of knowing that you have plenty of time to improve it. While you will later need to find the focus, at this stage it is advisable not to close off options or strive for perfection. You are exploring; some leads will work, others won't, but at this stage you can't say which is which.

As Anna's account indicated, there is no correct or proper starting point for a first draft. Any first sentence will work as long as you're not showing off or trying too hard. If you get stuck, there's no shame in breaking off to start a new section, to regain momentum. You don't need to know where your first draft is headed or where it will end, and if you imagine you do, you should suspend this expectation. You'll know when you reach the end: it will be at the point you say *Ah, so this is what my essay is.* It is more than likely that the end of the first draft will become the beginning of the essay.

If you're an incorrigible procrastinator, we suggest you acquire your first draft by staging the rush early, writing a draft as if it were an exam. If your problem is anxious over-reading, set yourself a firm reading deadline.

There are no mistakes in a first draft, so enjoy yourself and follow your interests.

Middle drafts

A journal is an opportunity to engage in a conversation with your own writing, and this is also the process that characterises middle drafts. Rather than being a tidying up of the first draft, they are an opportunity to take it further.

An analogy may help. To do a quick clean-up of your room, you remove from sight whatever seems embarrassing. In a thorough cleaning, though, you empty out every drawer and shelf. Even if the thorough cleaning starts as a chore, there is a pleasure in running your eyes over this forgotten but familiar material. There is pleasure too in the ideas that come to you about how it can be reordered.

The problem many students have is gaining access to the wardrobes and drawers of their first draft. They reread the draft and see nothing more to do with it. One way to shake this blasé attitude is to leave the first draft fallow. After a day or week, if you can read with new eyes, you will be able to add to the draft by applying techniques of secondary analysis. You might also do further reading and look over your journal again. At this stage your essay is still growing.

Through unpacking the contents of your first draft, you will gain a new appreciation of the bigger issues on which your essays leans, and you will need to refocus the essay accordingly. You will want to change starting points and conclusions, to cut some parts and expand others. If first draft words threaten to throw you from your new line, you may prefer to start writing again from scratch.

During these middle drafts, think carefully about what your readers need to be told. If you take for granted a step in the argument, if you don't call readers' attention to a significant implication, you cannot expect them to make the connection themselves. Only at this late stage are you becoming self-conscious about your essay-writing task, and by now your interesting ideas and the safety of words-already-on-the-page have calmed your sense of threat. You're probably having fun and looking forward to readers' responses.

The possibilities generated by thorough middle drafts are the real magic of writing in stages, as Lakma explains:

I had written what I thought was a decent draft. It had all the things I wanted to talk about, those things were interesting, therefore it would be a good thesis. I figured I only needed to fix it up and make it more academic or whatever. But when my supervisor read it, I knew that he wasn't happy with it, which annoyed and frustrated me because I couldn't see what was wrong. So I was in a real slump. The fact that I didn't know how to fix it made me hate it. It made me not want to look at it.

So I was reading through it and it was really frustrating me because it seemed I was saying the same thing over and over. It didn't read smoothly because ideas weren't followed through. They would just start and then trail into something else and then another point would be made that had sort of already been made but not actually followed through. It was like reading something that kept starting but not finishing any ideas properly or following them through to solid conclusions.

I was reading it and fixing bits and thinking that the bits I was fixing weren't actually making it any better because what it needed was a complete overhaul.
I was going crazy with frustration. It all seemed pointless.

And then suddenly I realised what I hadn't been able to get before, that I could do a complete overhaul and change the entire thing! It was amazing when I saw I could do that, and that I needed to take all the ideas that I rambled about a bit and then came back to later and I needed to make these ideas major themes and make them structured as complete ideas following through with a full argument and conclusion. This was what my supervisor had meant when he kept saying 'Yes, but what are the implications of this?' For some reason I hadn't been able to work an idea all the way through before.

When I was reading it and couldn't see what was wrong (and yet knew it wasn't right), I was attached to it, thinking I had done the right thing, and defensive of it. When I was unattached and saw it as something that wasn't me, *I could work with it again. What I had to do was take out all the topic headings that kept repeating themselves in different contexts and work out from the repetition what were the major themes I wasn't naming.*

I had read a tip that said to read over the draft lightly and look for key words that stand out. I wasn't able to read lightly when I was too attached and I already thought I knew what my keywords were. Nothing could help me when I thought I knew. But a lot of the revelation came from realising that I had to distinguish these themes. (Lakma)

Middle drafts make more mess before the cleaning up finally begins.

Final drafts

The work of tidying up an essay is generally counter-productive until the final draft. Even then this polishing is not simply decorative: it is a refining, a process of more clearly finding the essence of the essay.

Here are some things to consider:

- Go through the essay paragraph by paragraph, sentence by sentence, phrase by phrase and finally word by word, removing any repetition and sidetracks. This process will clarify the line of your argument, with each decision encouraging you to discover what is really important.
- A rule of thumb among editors is that writers must often sacrifice their favourite passages. These passages have been there to reassure you as you work through early drafts. Once you're in the final draft, they no longer have a role.
- Check that your sentences are sentences and that your paragraphs are paragraphs. A sentence is generally one unit of meaning, and a paragraph generally one step in an argument. If they're not right, then neither is the presentation of your argument.
- When you have a lively feel for the logic of your essay, consider whether readers need more explicit signposting. Are your titles and subheadings accurate and do they set the right tone? Do the introduction and conclusion do justice to the whole essay? Do readers need help in distinguishing the voice of the essay and the conjectural voices that the essay occasionally

presents? As a host, you must give readers enough information so they can feel at home in the essay.

- Read the essay aloud to yourself several times on different occasions. Is the rhythm pleasing or monotonous? This test will be the final check on your line. If you cannot find a form of words that sings, it's because you're clinging to unsuitable words or phrases.
- Consider the comfort and needs of your reader when laying out your pages for printing.

A final draft uses tests of presentation and style to clarify lines of argument.

READING

When students try to write essays in quick single drafts they are acting out the common assumption that writing is writing down – merely putting on paper the meanings and thoughts that are already present in the author's mind. According to this view, writing simply conveys the author's meaning without making a difference and without developing that meaning.

In the last chapter, by contrast, we emphasised the importance of the writing *process.* Writing itself can be creative, producing ideas and possibilities that the writer hasn't previously seen. Indeed, all writing contains possibilities unknown to the writer.

This argument affects how we read and understand reading. Rather than the recovery of a meaning put into the text by its author, reading is a creative engagement with the writer and text. If there is always more to a text than the author can know, we are contributing to the making of meaning whenever we read. Reading itself makes a difference.

Different ways of reading

The counterpart to the notion that writing is writing down is the notion that reading is comprehension – a meaning has been put into the text by the author and the task of the reader is to grasp this meaning. In this model, reading does not make a difference.

Comprehension is always a possible reading strategy, but if students don't realise that there are other ways of reading, they put themselves under pressure and distance themselves from their work. This is Kim:

> *Whenever I'm trying to grasp something new but just absolutely can't, I just give in to temptation and stop, using the excuse 'This is boring' or 'I'm bored!' If I really don't understand what I'm doing or reading, thus not relating to whatever I'm doing, it'll not be meaningful to me, hence the boredom sets in. (Kim)*

Kim's experience is common. Reading is a major source of complaint amongst university students: *There's too much. It is too hard. It is too easy. Can't this be said in a more straightforward way?* These complaints arise because reading is being treated as a comprehension test of the students' knowledge and they are afraid of failure: *Have I got it yet? Should I get a book out that explains this other book to me? Would I sound foolish if I told my tutor what I thought about the book?*

When students realise that the development of ideas at university relies on learning more creative reading skills, they often feel a renewed sense of possibility. You will recall Tian's experience from the chapter *Interest*, and here is Camilla's account of a similar shift:

> *So the question is, did Durkheim and Simmel work for me? Yes and no. I was definitely bored reading them. Bored, distracted, unwilling to engage. I am struggling to engage with a text. Not that I am an unwilling reader, because I'm a voracious reader. It's just the consciousness of sitting down with a book of readings and saying 'OK, today Simmel'. But then, in class, both*

lectures and tutorials, I really feel the engagement, I feel it between all the people, the text and the ideas buzzing around the room like flies ... it's really the text that I have problems with. Can't handle the closeness of the text. Or maybe I have to break my conventional learning moulds, and then my mind will be free from the shackles of comprehension, and I will be able to engage effectively with the text.

Oh, I just flicked open the book and read the preface, it's so nice. Isn't it funny how receptivity – like inspiration, comes unexpectedly. I have read this chapter before, as words on a page, as an amusing anecdote, vaguely identifying with it but taking absolutely nothing away from it. And for some reason, sitting here today, in the library, distracted, with a time limit, I read it and I get it. Strange – and wholly unexpected. Maybe I don't get it entirely; if a reading is an interaction between text and reader, which it undoubtedly is, then each 'getting it' will be different. (Camilla)

Notice how the same text can involve quite a different reading experience, depending on the way you're reading. Camilla only felt she understood it when she wasn't diverted by the pressure of comprehension.

This is how Camilla pursues the implications of this experience:

It's the 'us and them'ness of perception that is damaging to creativity. It might as well be us versus them or me versus everything. Me against the world, against the chapter, struggling against an unfair environment that demands that I shop, work, find the 'right' place to start.

> *But when you see yourself within the world the us & them, me & you boundary begins to blur. It becomes a collaboration of interacting aspects of the world. (Camilla)*

Camilla identifies the key issue when she distinguishes between struggling and collaborating with a text: what you learn from a text and about a text depends on the nature of your relationship with it.

University requires and teaches new ways of reading.

The *process* of reading

Learning comes through the *process* of reading, from the listening, sitting with and waiting, the notes, lists and speculations. It is through this process of engagement that new possibilities emerge and begin buzzing in the space between the reader and the text:

> *I think I've learnt heaps from just sitting with a reading in my course reader and not trying to control or understand every word of it, but to let some bits affect you and then you'll see the relation and understand it better. (Anika)*

This engaged reading practice is based on dialogue. We don't read to pin down a text but to keep the conversation going, to keep the text alive. This can only occur if we are careful and respectful with the text. But there can be no single or correct reading of any text, any more than there is a single or correct form of relationship with another person. Different people will form different relations with the same text, and each of these readings may be valuable, even if they are not commensurable.

The same person will read a text differently in different situations. By changing our attitude, or changing the context of our reading, we learn more about the text. Camilla said: 'Maybe I don't get it entirely; if a reading is an interaction between text and reader, which it undoubtedly is, then each "getting it" will be different.' A creative approach to reading assumes that each 'getting it' will be both incomplete and different. The text is interesting because it is always being rediscovered.

Because a collaborative reading is an intimate relation with a text, it puts the reader in the creative space that inspired the writer. Reading is itself a form of writing. If you read creatively, you will *want* to write.

The text will help you if you let it.

Practical suggestions

Here are some practical implications of a collaborative understanding of reading.

- Nearly all of your readings will require more than one go: you're not expected to be able to 'get' them immediately. Leave yourself time to relax with the text. Read it again after the lecture and tutorial and see how much more you understand.
- Many people find it helpful to do a quick first reading to get an overall sense of the text, followed by a slower reading that focuses on specific passages of interest. Subsequent slow readings deepen appreciation.
- Don't get stuck on unfamiliar words. Get a sense of the meaning from the context, or look up a dictionary, or float over the word and move on.
- Because course readers are common today, students often don't have the chance to fall in love with books. Take time to browse around the library and bookshops. See what books and journals you come across. If you have enjoyed a reading in your course reader, borrow a book by that author.
- Don't postpone your reading of classic texts. You can always learn something from a text, using whatever competencies you have.
- Being open with texts doesn't mean you have to agree with them. Some of the most productive readings come through disagreement. But be respectful and patient in your disagreement, because the texts that

students start off hating are often those from which they learn most.

- You will read more skillfully if you're writing in a journal. As Belinda says:

  The workbook makes the readings a lot easier to handle. You can go through slowly and write what speaks to you. I found quite often that a few weeks after reading something and writing about it in the workbook, I could go back to the reading and understand a lot more of it. I found this to be especially true of writers who did not work for me at all the first time ... Even the readings that were not so easy carried ideas that made me think (even if those thoughts were sometimes a little off-track). (Belinda)

- Whenever you feel stuck, remember that reading is a relationship. Ask 'What is my relation with this text?' This question will get the reading going again.

Reading is a skill that people are always learning.

THINKING

I feel like I've learnt to think – almost like a waking up. I've learnt to discover what I think instead of making vague half guesses. (Camilla)

At university, learning how to think is as important as acquiring a body of knowledge. Knowledge is always growing and changing, but if your attitudes and thinking processes are open and effective, familiarity with changing subject matter looks after itself.

While each discipline has a specialist vocabulary, there are common terms used to describe thinking processes and methods. We're going to discuss some of these key terms here. However, it is important to bear in mind that these terms are continually being questioned and reformulated. The account that follows is not definitive.

Analysis

Analysis is usually described as the intellectual operation of breaking an entity into its fundamental elements.

The human body, for example, might be broken into brain, blood, bones and so on. Knowledge of a totality, it is assumed, can be derived from understanding these simpler parts.

This assumes, of course, that entities are finite and knowable. But entities can always be known in different ways through different connections. It is through these connections that knowledge develops.

By returning to its etymology, we can find a way to rethink analysis. Rather than a violent process of breaking and splitting, analysis means to loosen. To loosen is to find the room for play, to reduce pressure and density, to enhance fluency and possibility. Etymologically, to loosen is also to lose: analysis is a process of losing our certainties about what we know so that we can rediscover how things go together in the world.

Argument

In your essays you will be required to 'develop an argument'. This doesn't mean being argumentative or adversarial, though some disciplines may ask you to engage in adversarial types of argument. It means you are pursuing a line of thought by asking a sequence of rigorous questions, proposing an idea and following through its implications.

In Chapter 5, *Writing*, Lakma described learning how to argue. She could tell the first draft of her thesis wasn't developing an argument because it was simultaneously 'saying the same thing over and over' and starting ideas that would 'trail into something else, without anything being followed through to conclusions'.

Conclusions to an argument should not be regarded as final. They are simply the result of having followed a line of thinking as far as you can, for now, in this context.

The best, most creative, conclusions are those that open up new questions and new lines of investigation.

Classification

Classification is a fundamental process in the generation of knowledge, so basic that many students and teachers take it for granted. It produces the familiar sense of separate things each having a proper place in the world: here is a cat, there is a dog, and this is me, a human. However, when we take classification systems as given, we overlook the processes that have produced these separations.

Cultural competence requires the improvisation of pathways through a limitless series of overlapping classification systems. Nothing belongs to one class alone. For example, a human is a human *and* a primate *and* a mammal.

Classifications are transformation systems, allowing the movement of meanings up, down and across the system's organised grid. Things are not simply themselves; with a simple shift of angle everything is something else, something more specific, more general, alike or contiguous in some way, its meaning located somewhere else. It is through these classificatory processes that knowledge grows.

Concepts

Concepts can be used either to define objects or to open up new connections. They can be thought of as an answer or as an intellectual tool that facilitates understanding. An example illustrates the difference.

Suppose you are thinking about architectural styles and decide to apply the concept 'baroque'. You might use this concept as a way of defining a building: *This is what this is – it's baroque!* In this case, a concept has become a label that concludes the discussion. Alternatively, you could ask: *Does this building have some of the qualities associated with baroque? Are there discrepant elements? What other concepts might be brought into play? What can I learn from this, about this building and about the concept of baroque?* If you adopt this kind of approach you are putting concepts and things into a dialogue that keeps the learning process moving.

It's useful to remember the etymology of the word 'concept': conceive, conception: imagine, become pregnant. Concepts produce new possibilities. If you get stuck in your thinking, you can ask, 'What concept might take the thinking further?'

Critical thinking

Critical thinking is universally valued at university. It is sometimes taken to mean being judgmental and negative, but at university the emphasis is placed on the importance of acknowledging differences.

Viewed in this way, critical thinking has some of the following connotations: questioning assumptions, especially your own; rigorous thinking; careful, considered, convincing argument; pursuing implications; pushing ideas beyond the current boundaries; not accepting the orthodoxies of the discipline; making new connections. Critical thinking is close to creative thinking.

Description

The term description is often paired with 'analysis'. For example, you might be asked to 'describe and analyse' or you might find a comment on your essay 'too descriptive,

insufficient analysis'. When teachers say this they imply that you are not putting the description to work conceptually. In other words, you are not *really* thinking.

Comments like these may make it appear that description and analysis are separate, but there are always some conceptual assumptions involved in description. Your task is to identify and develop them.

You might ask: 'Why did I describe x in this way rather than that? What were my underlying assumptions? What issues are raised by this description? How is this description pertinent to the argument that I am developing?' By identifying the analytic element of description, you develop your ideas.

Detachment

Detachment is valued in objective approaches to knowledge. To see the object as it truly is, 'by itself', the observer must have a detached eye.

Detachment is regarded as a corrective to its opposite, attachment, which is taken to be the basis of subjective knowledge. The attached person has identified with the object under analysis, so that when they look at it, they see and respond to the reflection of themselves.

There is a third possibility, based on non-attachment. A way of knowing based on dialogue and interest, non-attachment avoids the either/or of subjectivity/objectivity without denying these as ways of knowing.

Detached knowledge claims to know *about* the other; attached knowledge claims we can only know ourselves. In non-attached modes I know *with* you. I learn about difference through relationship.

Dialogue

Socrates is the most famous teacher in Western history because of his claim that learning derives from dialogue and not from a passing of knowledge from teacher to student.

An influential account of dia-logic is offered by the physicist David Bohm:

> *The weekend began with the expectation that there would be a series of lectures and informative discussions with emphasis on content. It gradually emerged that something more important was actually involved – the awakening of*

> *the process of dialogue itself as a free flow of meaning among all the participants. In the beginning, people were expressing fixed positions, which they were tending to defend, but later it became clear that to maintain the feeling of friendship in the group was much more important than to hold any position. Such friendship has an impersonal quality in the sense that its establishment does not depend on a close personal relationship between participants. A new kind of mind thus begins to come into being which is based on the development of a common meaning that is constantly transforming in the process of dialogue. People are no longer primarily in opposition, nor can they said to be interacting, rather they are participating in this pool of common meaning which is capable of constant development and change. In this development the group has no pre-established purpose, though at each moment a purpose that is free to change may reveal itself. The group thus begins to engage in a new dynamic relationship in which no speaker is excluded, and in which no particular content is excluded ... going further along these lines would open up the possibility of transforming not only the relationship between people, but even more, the very nature of consciousness in which these relationships arise.*

The principle of dialogue is just as applicable to reading and writing as to tutorials and lectures.

Explication

At university we strive to make things explicit, spelling out our arguments, leaving nothing unsaid. We try to identify the things we are analysing, and perhaps try to count and classify them. But there's more going on in explication than many people realise, for the explicit always presumes an implicit. There are always further implications.

The composer Debussy remarked that music is found between the notes, and we could also say that meaning is dispersed between the words and lines on the page. A reader who cannot read between the lines is a reader unable to enter the text.

Perhaps elaborated texts are valued not because they aspire toward a total understanding of the things of the world, but because the elaboration gives us a greater appreciation of what cannot be said. Perhaps we value an elaborated argument because it augments our feel for the inchoate possibilities behind it.

Frameworks

Academics talk a lot about the need for theoretical and conceptual frameworks. Often frameworks are taken as grids, superimposed on phenomena to fix their classificatory position. The more important function of frameworks, however, is to help us focus on what is special about any phenomenon.

Have you ever noticed the difference between a framed and an unframed view, the difference, say, between looking at the ocean through trees and looking at it with no visual interruption? In the former case, the ocean comes closer to you, you can feel the colours and textures and sounds more clearly, you can feel the ocean's presence. Without a frame, there is something more unfocused about the sight.

Likewise, if you come to a book without implicit framing questions, nothing will stand out for you. Without initial concerns, no *new* concerns can emerge. Thus frames work in a transformative manner, allowing us to see things differently, to see the same ocean, or the same book, with new eyes.

Rigour

Rigour normally indicates strict adherence to the rules of proper scholarly or scientific procedure, but the term deserves a broader interpretation. Rigour implies our responsibility to ask more and more questions of the world in which we participate, our responsibility to avoid the deadening effects of becoming attached to a fixed view of truth.

In this usage, rigour isn't simply a mechanism for arriving at the truth through the use of proper and reliable methods. It is a matter of continually letting go of what we think we know in order to find truth all over again.

Wholistic thinking

'Wholistic' comes from the word whole, which can be usefully distinguished from 'total'. Totals and wholes are two ways of thinking: a total is the sum of the parts, whereas a whole is greater than the sum of the parts.

When knowledge is concerned with the total, it studies the parts as separate identities, taking the total to be a bounded entity. Knowledge concerned with wholes focuses on relations and connections, assuming that specific forms emerge through relations.

Total implies the possibility of a definitive knowledge; a whole involves a notion of the continuous unfolding of possibilities, only some of which are recognised within the total.

When thinkers want to know the total, they don't include themselves in the knowledge. A wholistic approach recognises our participation in the world and in knowledge processes. It is as participants that we understand the whole.

ASSESSMENT

Grades

I remember when I did my Higher School Certificate I wasn't at all interested in what I had learnt. We had pretty much covered all the information in the curriculum by the beginning of year 12, and then it was all a matter of continuously revising the same material, trying to memorise as much as possible. I wasn't learning anything new and I became completely detached and disinterested in my work right through year 12. When the trials came around, the fear of failure was the only thing that made me study in the end. It paid off. I got great marks. But my educational experience was far from enjoyable. I did it because I 'had to' – you can't get into uni and further expand your horizons until you've got through the HSC. It's a shame really but that's the way the education system works. (Rachel)

Students regret that a grade in a final high school exam comes to dominate learning at school. This is why they arrive at university hoping for educational experiences that are more engaged than the ones that qualified them for tertiary education. Even so, university represents a step into the unknown, and many students become scared when university offers them the possibilities they've hoped for. Listen to Vicky's experience:

> *After reading the outlines provided in the handout mentioning 'creativity' and 'ideas', I felt myself getting so tense that I had to slump on the couch to watch Jerry Springer for an hour. Why is uni never clear-cut? It's easier said than done to clear your mind from teachers' and markers' expectations, because when it comes down to the crunch, my final mark is what is constantly at the back of my mind. So it is true that my final mark is my goal, and I don't think I should block that out completely. However I do understand also that in focusing on the big goal all the time, I miss what's in-between. Although I understand this concept, or way of thinking, that has been mentioned not only in this lecture but as a whole motto for uni and even school, I'm not going to lie to you by saying that I have miraculously changed the habits I've held for a lifetime in a week. (Vicky)*

Because grading does not simply go away at university, students cannot expect a miracle to change their learning habits. Nevertheless, university *does* offer a greater array of assessment forms than the final school exam, and *does* offer far greater respect for creativity and ideas. And because of this it does offer students the chance to learn the learning skills that will prepare them for life outside educational institutions.

A first step is a realistic appreciation of what grades offer. Grades are a way of measuring knowledge, of turning uniquely different qualities into numbers for the purpose of comparison and ranking. All grading systems filter knowledge in the process of measuring it. Rather than being evaluated on their knowledge, students are being tested on the subsets of that knowledge that are accessible through particular evaluation techniques, selected as much for bureaucratic as pedagogic reasons.

A preoccupation with grades, then, is an unreliable guide to the success of an educational process. Rather than serving as the point of education, they are best treated as one among the many forms of feedback available at university.

This shift in focus will ensure a richer learning experience, and is also likely to improve your grades! Ask a pianist or gymnast preparing for examination: the more aware they are of judgment, the more their performance suffers from self-consciousness. Inspired performance requires a strange mixture of tension and relaxation that cannot be found if you're performing with the expectation of a critic's praise or condemnation.

Look toward the education and the grades will take care of themselves.

Criticism and praise

At university you will be getting constant feedback on your work, from teachers and fellow students. Some of this feedback will come as written comments on essays, some will be given orally in tutorials and consultations and coffee-shop discussions with friends. Some will feel positive, some will not. If you avoid becoming defensive about critical comments, and avoid becoming dependent on positive comments, this feedback will be a major source of learning at university.

Feedback on your work is a form of dialogue that allows others to teach you about qualities in the work that you hadn't yourself noticed. The sensitive commentator has the fresh insight of an outsider, and yet seems to know the work's potential more intimately than you do yourself. Accordingly, dialogue allows an educational process where knowledge is simultaneously coming to you and growing from you. This is the quality at play whenever education is engaging.

Defensiveness is a major obstacle to this flow of dialogue, so if a colleague or a teacher criticises your work, don't take it personally. They have been asked to talk about your work, not about *you*. When you react defensively, you cannot hear the suggestions that might help you develop your skills and ideas. Moreover, you are likely to feel defensive about precisely those parts of your work that, deep down, you know need attention. Knowing this, you can convert your defensiveness to creative use. The times when you don't want to hear someone's response to your work are the times when you have the most to gain by listening.

The advantage of staying open in the face of critical comments is straight-forward, but why shouldn't you take positive feedback personally? Praise may initially give you energy, but interest wanes when it is performed for external rewards. Dimitra tells us about this problem:

> *Last year when I embarked on the first year of my architecture degree, I found that many aspects of my week were generally more personally confronting than*

I expected them to be. We would design/research our work and always have to present and pin up each week at least 2-3 times for all the subjects. Then the tutors would question aspects of people's work and make comparisons between work that was more successful than the rest and why. Our work seems somehow so tangibly connected to us that a slander against our work is an affliction on us, on who we are: a judgment, a trial. I think I was battling this on two fronts: the first, being a perfectionist, and the obvious second, defining myself through the eyes of others, and in this case through the tutors and lecturers.

My sister, who is a year ahead and also in architecture, said 'Try and learn to detach from your work. Try and not take to heart every word they say.' So I tried but I found I was trying harder in another way to avoid the desperate situation again. That was to work harder on the work itself! To make it so good that I may be able to avoid harsh criticism in front of peers that I felt may be inwardly laughing at me. And in this attempt to make things flawless I occasionally succeeded and felt better. The High Distinctions came rolling in but there was a very strange reality creeping in.

The discomfort that followed stemmed from me realising that I was happier only when others were happy with me, with my work, my achievements. I realised that the compliments I was receiving were the basis of the attitude I had towards myself throughout the week: happy – sad – pride – shame. I had no idea how empty and fooled it had made me feel. I was an empty object waiting to be constantly filled. (Dimitra)

Don't take criticism *or* praise personally.

Fear of failure

When Rachel lost her interest at school, she relied for her motivation on a fear of failure. The same reliance prevails at university when students and lecturers are attached to grades and rankings. Yet as students explain, this is a destructive form of energy.

> *The pressure to do well is practically unbearable now. What should I do? I feel like bursting into tears each time I think about it and I know it is interfering with my actual learning in the course. I don't want to fail. (Alice)*

> *I'm constantly telling myself and other people that uni is nothing, that I don't do any work and I don't really care. It's my fear of failure motivating me to say these things. (Katrina)*

> *I find that when an essay is due I fear so much that I will try my hardest and only get a credit that I leave my essay to the absolute last minute. By doing this I think to myself: 'I've done all I can do, now let's see what mark I get.' Then if I get a credit I think to myself 'imagine what you could*

> *have got if you had started earlier', while also thinking, 'it's what you deserve for starting so late.' However it never changes the way I do things. With the next essay the same old cycle begins again. (Belinda)*

Katrina and Belinda are engaging in self-handicapping. A self-handicap is a prepared alibi, made in anticipation of a failure that the alibi makes more likely. By holding themselves back, students miss out on the possible joys of university, but at least they have something to blame in the event of the failure.

One way of dealing with the fear of failure is to remain focused on realistic possibilities of success. Only one student can top any course, but every student in every course can aspire to improve their previous marks. Moreover, students can usefully break the overall tasks into smaller units and thereby monitor their success in smaller and more realistic increments (I'm aiming to take good lecture notes today, I'm aiming to write an effective essay introduction).

These strategies are useful, yet they implicitly endorse the assumption that university is a matter of success or failure. A better idea is to shift the focus a stage further, from successful outcomes to fascination with the process.

When students are engaged in their work, they aren't cast low even if they receive lower marks than expected. They submit work knowing the risks they've taken and knowing that grading success can never be assured. Even if they'd known the grade outcome, they might not have betrayed the joy of their work.

Enjoy your studies and you cannot fail.

Perfectionism

Perfectionism is pervasive at university. Here is Jessica:

> *Growing up, academic success was paramount. Tortured by self-doubt and insecurity, I had an insatiable hunger for approval and recognition. Competition, ambition and perseverance fuelled a sense of accomplishment and self-worth. If I received a good mark, elation would follow; radiating with pride, I would convince myself that I was a good person, capable of anything. And if a mark proved fatal, it could be devastating to my sense of self, producing prolonged periods of doubt, depression, anxiety. (Jessica)*

Perfectionist students say they love their work. It is all that matters to them. Yet these students rarely hand in their work on time, and their work is frequently less rich than they had led the lecturer to expect.

Typically, what perfectionist students love is the fantasy they have of their work. They so idealise their love-object that they cannot relate to the messiness of the particular page of writing awaiting them on their desk. They swing between confidence and despair, as they shift between fantasies of success and fantasies of failure.

The problem of perfectionism is that its high standards are not of this world. This insight came to Jessica as a revelation. Having become attached to future achievements, she had lost her sense of joy and passion: *I found that I was no longer asking questions or being inquisitive about the world.* Once she let go of her perfectionism,

> *the inhibition, fear and insecurity which had plagued me disappeared. I was released into a world of possibility and discovery. I looked at everything with fresh eyes and a clear mind. (Jessica)*

Likewise, Dimitra found that engagement was the remedy for her perfectionism. Her crisis came when she became *really, really, really sick* with two stress-induced autoimmune diseases. No longer able to ignore the real problem – *how empty and void I was of real love* – Dimitra responded by becoming involved in extra-curricular areas of university life. It was netball, soccer and touch football that reminded her of:

> *the wonderful feeling of being with a group of people who are working with you and not against you. Friends, not foes; and you can be your own best friend and not worst enemy. It was okay to miss a goal. Self criticism was brought under control in this atmosphere. My best friend in Architecture and I would examine assignments and lecture material and site visits in terms of learning experience. Our learning journey, not the marks.(Dimitra)*

Loving her work rather than taking it personally, Dimitra found she no longer treated assessment as a fearful test of her perfection.

> *In the last major project, I smiled during the crit; I felt as if the tension had all disappeared or at least transformed. I was not the scrutinised item on the wall. I was having a meaningful conversation with the tutor about what was on the wall and the object was not me nor the work. I felt there was no longer an object – there was a series of happenings, opportunities, acknowledgements. (Dimitra)*

If you're kind to your work, you can be kind to yourself.

STUDENTS

Students arrive at university excited about the prospect of encountering new people and making new friends. But university is often not the passionate, chatty, witty, friendly place they imagined.

> *I was looking forward to meeting all sorts of new people, but then felt so overwhelmed when I got there. Where do you begin? How do you meet people in such a big place? You don't just go up to someone and say 'hi'.*

> *In Medicine, you go through with the same people, but in Arts there are different people in every class.*

> *Everyone else seems to have friends. What is the matter with me? I don't want to look like a lonely person. Where will I eat my lunch, when everyone else is eating with their friends? Everyone will see that I am alone.*

The above statements were made by senior students who had volunteered to mentor first year students. Most volunteered because they wanted to offer new students some of the support that they had missed. In the mentoring process, they told us, they found support themselves.

Friendship

Here is Anna, who found that friendship was the main issue confronting her upon arrival at university:

> *I think my biggest shock on coming to uni was not the new lecture styles and having to walk around a huge area and find things on my own, but rather the horrific fact that, somehow, I was not finding people whom I could imagine being good friends with. One moment I'm sure I've made a good friend at uni. I think this is them. Then the next day it's changed and I've changed my mind. (Anna)*

Because finding friends seems a matter of choice, it feels arbitrary to Anna, but it is also arduous because of the number of choices and the weight each carries. Anna recounts a story which tells how her problem was solved:

> *The other week, a girl from uni was really upset. I noticed other people saying 'Call me if you need to talk' and it just struck me as so stupid because of course she needed to talk! That was just a way to make them feel like they'd done their bit.*
>
> *So that night I called her at home. It was the first time I had ever called anyone from uni. About a week later I got a note from her saying how thankful she was and she didn't know what she'd do without me as a friend. The fact is, I didn't really feel like I had done anything. (Anna)*

Rather than dwelling on her own loneliness, Anna spontaneously called someone in distress. She wasn't aiming to turn this girl into her friend, but her generosity gave her friendship.

It's the stupid, insignificant things you do together that creates the bond. When I ring up my best friends, I don't do it for a reason; I do it so we can share each other's experiences. (Anna)

Friendships arise but cannot be produced.

Competition

Why is it difficult to stay open with those whom we meet at university? A major reason is the prevalence on campus of competition, and the reason for this, in turn, is that so many staff and students are preoccupied with defending themselves from perceived attack. When you compare yourself with others, you turn them into rivals.

I compared myself to others who did better and this just accentuated my feelings of failure. (Natalia)

The only reason I haven't finished my thesis is because I couldn't bear to do a stupid conventional one, like Karen did. Anyone could finish a thesis if that was all you did. I'm better than that. (Paul)

Lisa is [my supervisor's] favourite student. It's so obvious. It makes me feel sick to watch the two of them together.

But she'd better watch out because every year so far he's changed his favourite. Put a foot wrong and he'll act like he has nothing to do with you. (Mary)

I remembered an audition in which I was relaxed and did well in improvisation and another audition when I did poorly. I realised that I let go when I did the good audition and got called-back. It was at the call-back that I compared myself to those other call-back actors around me instead of enjoying interacting with the script and people and having fun with it. I found myself getting jealous of all those others actors' talent and the more I put them on a pedestal, the more nervous and inadequate I felt and the less chance I could interact with them on stage in front of the director: 'I'm *shit,* so I'm *not going to do any good'. (Vicky)*

If this competition is part of the environment, it leads to a falseness in people's relationships.

For example, people who are afraid to talk openly to one another sidle into conversation on the basis of shared enmities. It might be scorn for the student in the tutorial who talks too much, or it might be criticism of the lecturer for wasting your time.

There was another guy who did an economics course with me, who would corner me after each tutorial to say what a load of rubbish it all was, that the real world was nothing like the way it was being described in these classes, that he'd dropped out once before and was thinking he'd probably drop out again. (Luke)

As Luke goes on to explain, shared enmities don't produce genuine friendships:

> *I never really had much of anything to say to him; I'd listen patiently, ask him some question, but I didn't know what to say back. In part I agreed with his assessment, but I still wanted to learn how to do it 'their' way. I didn't know how to say that to him, though, and I don't know if it would have gone anywhere if I had. (Luke)*

The collective attribution of blame often becomes obsessive, but no amount of blame can remedy the damage done by hostile and fearful relations with our peers. These relations deny those qualities that make each of us incomparable, and our relationships and learning experiences suffer from this denial.

Comparison leads to competition.

Generosity and collaboration

People cannot confirm their special skills and talents through competition. Unique qualities only become manifest through relationships. Vicky explains this when continuing the story of her auditions:

> *I had to get myself in the right frame of mind by going over in my head the dynamics of performance which fosters creativity rather than fear and self-consciousness:*

to include the audience and director and other actors and space as all part of a performance and to know it's not just up to me – that if ideas come they will come, if they don't they don't. It's like training your body for a physical activity. My attitude constantly kept reverting back to a self-focus, but repetition and persistence allowed me to really enjoy the audition. After that audition, it didn't matter to me whether I did or didn't get a part. (Vicky)

What Vicky says of acting applies throughout university life. For example, the tutorials that students value are invariably those where competition is minimised, where the lively disagreement lacks rivalry.

I really enjoy our tutorials. I can talk about ideas without being nervous or self-conscious. The way the group works, people listen closely to each other and respond openly. We're all contributing to the discussion, even the students who aren't saying much. We come out of the class wanting to go on talking. (Jeremy)

In our tutorials people helped each other to understand rather than relying completely on the tutor. I think each of us gained from that experience. The tutorial allowed me to grow as a person. (Tanya)

My favourite aspect of this course was the essay process discussion in tutorials. I truly believe that doing this process has helped my essay become a lot better than it could have been. It was great having a small group look over what I was doing while I did the same for them. I even enjoyed the process of editing, regardless of whether my tips were taken (Belinda)

To be most yourself, work openly and collaboratively.

Rushing around and hanging out

> *When walking across the university, everything around me becomes an object, even those hundreds of students who are walking beside me. I do not aim at seeing them as objects, but the pressure from assignments always controls my mind. Once I step into the uni, I cannot stop thinking what books should I borrow for my linguistics assignment? Have I downloaded the notes for the international business? All of these questions make me become blind, so I cannot see how good the weather is and what the passer-bys are doing. Everything is an object. (Jasmin)*

Because students who are always rushing around are living in the future, they can never 'be there' when others need them. Their purposes turn others into either potential obstacles or advantageous contacts and such objectification precludes lively relationships.

To make friends you need time free of purpose. More bluntly, you need to find ways of just hanging out with other students. Lakma makes this point:

I miss school because of the guaranteed meeting of friends five consecutive days of the week. It doesn't matter so much who your friends are, because, when you are a child, the people you hang out with is a result of forces largely beyond your control. What counts is that you see them every day and pass innumerable hours with them. Quantity time with friends is quality time.

Sitting around, hanging around, doing nothing, playing around: it doesn't matter what you do, what matters is that it is completely un-tense. This is the setting in which bonds are formed and friendships are made.

When you leave school, friendships require maintenance. Not only do we require the excuse of a beverage – coffee, tea, alcohol – to meet someone, we also require organisation. Where we once had to be there anyway, we now have to phone and organise the social interaction. We meet for two hours, and then go back to our separate lives. It has suddenly become awkward to say to people we like 'Let's just hang out together.' We offer coffee rather than offer ourself openly, because we don't quite know if we're worthy. (Lakma)

While university might not offer as stable a hanging out environment as school, there are nonetheless opportunities available to students who aren't always rushing around.

In some faculties, for example, students find themselves within cohorts that share courses, that have their own lecture-theatres and libraries, and that have workloads requiring long hours on campus. These students may not think of searching for friends. There is an institutionalised hanging out.

If you're not in a faculty with a well-organised cohort, what can you do?

You can certainly consider joining some of the clubs and societies on campus, knowing that you'll be putting yourself in a situation where friendships may form while you're busy doing something else. Volunteers are always welcome, so, if you can, help out.

If you are in a faculty like arts or sciences, you could regard the tutorials and the group projects as safe and structured opportunities for hanging out with other students. Get involved. Be generous. Tutorials always need your help.

We must, however, end with a warning. Hanging out leads to friendships, but that is not its purpose. It is its own reward. An interesting course is *itself* supportive, whether or not it leads to personal friendships. You may find that these friendly but not intimate relationships give you all the sense of care, involvement and respect that you need.

Get involved.

TEACHERS

Most of us can recall teachers who have changed our lives. Certain teachers arrive to teach us just what we need to know just when we need to know it. They are the path to knowledge. But this is a path that students and teachers must make together.

University teachers regard students not as dependents but as people who share with them a passion for knowledge. Assuming that students *want* to learn, lecturers trust them to organise their own work, and, after the disciplines of school, students usually welcome this responsibility. Part of this responsibility is care for the relationships on which university depends. Teaching and learning can be effective only if students recognise the essential role that they have to play in this process, only if both students and teachers respond to the needs of their relationship.

What teachers do

Just as good teachers must continually remind themselves of the students' perspective, good students need to know how situations appear to teachers. This can be difficult for students because they haven't been academics. It will help you, then, to know what teachers do at university:

- Research and write in their particular field. Deliver conference papers. Send articles to journals for consideration through anonymous peer review. Write book proposals for publishers' consideration. Academics are expected to publish at a steady rate throughout their careers.

- Manage research projects. This might include: writing grant application proposals; coordinating colleagues in research teams; supervising research assistants and PhD students working on a project.
- Review articles submitted to journals for possible publication.
- Read and comment on the work in progress of peers and colleagues.
- Supervise honours and PhD students. This includes regular consultations and reading and commenting on work in progress and drafts.
- Undertake consultancies, and provide expert advice to organisations in the public and private sectors.
- Undertake service to the discipline and the profession. This can include: serving on editorial boards of journals; running conferences; sitting on accreditation committees; holding consultancies and joint appointments.
- Undertake administration at university, faculty, school, department or course level. Most academics do some school administration and nearly all undertake course administration, which involves: tutorial allocation; timetabling; finding suitable rooms; ordering books for bookshops and the library; keeping student records; coordinating tutors.
- Liaise with staff. Teachers meet frequently to coordinate their teaching and share teaching strategies.

- Mark students' work: reading and providing feedback on essays; grading and examining; entering results; attending examiners' meetings.
- Prepare lectures and tutorials.
- Give lectures and tutorials.
- Plan new courses and revise old ones.
- Select and prepare readings for course readers.
- Undertake student consultations.
- Report on career development.

Two points arise from this list.

First, there are many hours of invisible teaching work for every hour spent in the classroom. You should feel free to approach teachers, but don't take it personally if they aren't in their offices when you knock. It doesn't mean they don't want to help you, only that they have other commitments as well. If they're not available when you call, make an appointment.

Second, academics are always learning, and always having their work evaluated. Students and teachers are not opposites. When students and teachers recognise what they have in common as well as their differences, they work together more harmoniously.

Student-teacher relations need care and respect.

Teaching and learning

Since teachers are always learning, they are not imparting a final knowledge when they are teaching. The best teachers are those who teach students how to learn. And, conversely, a good student is one who teaches the teacher how to teach.

This idea has a long history in Western thought, traditionally being traced back to Socrates: 'I am not teaching … anything, but all I do is question.'

To show what this principle implies, let's imagine a typical moment in student-teacher relations. A student preparing for an essay is consulting his tutor about his initial thoughts. 'So what have you got in mind?', the tutor asks. While the student talks, the tutor listens closely, but she's not so much trying to catch the student's meaning as allow it to work on her. She's as interested in his tone and gestures as his words.

When the student finishes, the tutor asks him to elaborate on certain words or themes that struck her as being significant, or to identify what is *most* important to him, or to think out loud about this or that connection. The student isn't sure what the tutor is getting at, or *if* the tutor is getting at anything, but her queries have given him fresh ideas and he answers each question openly, following it wherever it takes him.

Both student and teacher are excited by this conversation. Things are happening. By the end it is clear that the student's initial formulation wasn't in accord with his interests. It was too stiff, too general, trying too hard to impress. The conversation has focused the question, making it more manageable but also more resonant with the student's deepest concerns. 'How did you know that was what I really wanted to write about?' the student would like to ask, but the teacher would deny having had such knowledge. All she did was ask the questions that occurred to her.

Through this dialogue, both student and teacher are learning and teaching. The tutor's questions are guided by what the student offers.

She is asking genuine questions, not working from a pre-given script or toward a pre-established conclusion. When these questions take the student deeper into his thinking, the teacher also learns more about the topic.

Nothing would have been learned from this consultation if tutor and student had regarded each other as opposites, one with and one without knowledge.

To make this point, let's imagine how the situation might have gone. Here are three scenarios.

In the first, the student announces that he can find nothing to say. He needs help. What should he write about? When the tutor asks about his interests, he responds blankly and repeats his request for instructions.

In the second, the teacher disregards the student's thoughts and gives him a mini-lecture that ends with a suggested topic and reading list and clues to the proper interpretation.

In the third situation, the student is eager to show that he already knows all the answers. He fends off the tutor's questions as if they are challenges to his ability and knowledge.

Creative dialogue is impossible in these situations because student and teacher are not listening and responding to each other. They have assumed that the consultation and essay are demonstrations of existing knowledge rather than opportunities for developing new ideas.

Enter openly into dialogue with your teachers.

Responsibility

I had never before actually considered a classroom scenario through the eyes of the teacher. (Rossella)

Students are sometimes affronted by the idea that teachers are primarily learners. You can hear them thinking: *I don't believe you! What right do you have to be teaching us then?*

By locating all responsibility with teachers, this attitude avoids recognition of the responsibility that students share. Think of the student who requested his tutor's help but had nothing himself to offer. By putting the tutor on a pedestal, he is losing respect for both himself and the tutor. He loses respect for himself because he knows he is avoiding any responsibility for the learning process. And he loses respect for the tutor by placing her in an impossible situation with his resentful demand: *you're the one supposed to know so you fix it; I'm not responsible here.*

So what is the responsibility of students? How do students teach teachers?

- First, by showing teachers what students need for learning. Teachers rely on honest feedback to improve their courses and teaching. This commentary and questioning is not a last resort used when the teacher fails: it is the basis of the good teacher's success.
- Second, by explaining what they don't understand, students teach teachers what they need to be teaching. Teachers are grateful for apparently naïve questions. It is often in answering these questions that they rediscover the basic principles informing their own work.
- Third, students teach teachers through dialogue in tutorials, essays and journals. Whenever an idea comes to life for students, through the specific connections they make, teachers learn about that idea anew.

Teachers need you.

Respect and trust

You can see from our imagined consultations that respectful dialogue does not rely on students and teachers being the same as each other. Both have responsibilities but not the same ones. The teacher has two primary responsibilities.

The first is to facilitate dialogue, retaining an awareness of the process itself. Teachers must provide the safe learning space where participants feel they can be open and unselfconscious. It follows that while teachers and students talk openly, they are not like best friends. Their relationship doesn't call for self-disclosure or familiarity. On the contrary, a certain impersonality diminishes self-consciousness and allows a trusting environment where participants don't need to feel like favourites in order to feel welcome.

The teacher's second responsibility is to demonstrate or model the skills in reading, writing and learning that students are trying to develop. In our imagined consultation, for example, the tutor's most valuable lesson was her practical demonstration of how to hold questions open.

Teachers cannot fulfil their responsibilities without students' trust. Teachers know that certain practices are effective, but they cannot tell students exactly what will come from these practices. At key points students need to suspend their desire for known outcomes and recognise that they cannot progress on the basis of fully-informed choice. Trusting their teachers, they must *be with* the tasks that the teachers assign.

Here is an example. When a PhD student felt lost, unsure of the direction his thesis should take, his supervisor set him the task of writing an A4 page every day and emailing it to him. All the student had to do was write; the content was unimportant. At the end of the year, the student wrote to the supervisor:

> *It's been a tremendous time for me – not only have I learned an enormous amount, but I've been rediscovering a joy in reading and writing that I'd forgotten I'd lost. (Celal)*

Because the student trusted the supervisor and the discipline of the daily task, he was free to learn without anxiety. The discipline proved to be liberating and creative.

Mutual trust and respect produce safe learning environments.

TIME

Too much time and too little time

University students are normally given plenty of time in which to write essays and study for exams. They are then required to organise their own work routines and study plans. It is at this point that time becomes a problem:

> *Everyone knows they should spread out their workload, but as so often happens, I still wait until dangerously close to the due date before getting started. Why is it so difficult to get going, especially when there is a considerable time gap between now and the due date? (Tian)*

Overwhelmed with a sense of too *much* time, students procrastinate with the unconscious aim of running out of time:

> *When you have plenty of time on your hands, sometimes you become very strict on the excellence of the writing. Therefore not being hard on yourself comes from running out of time. (Justine)*

Although Justine says that procrastination stops you being hard on yourself, she recognises that running out of time is also punishing. She talks of being stressed and exhausted with procrastination by the time she gets to her work. Another student, Christine, says:

Pressure is literally this crowding in. You feel overwhelmed, claustrophobic, in fact. You feel like you are being bombarded all the time. Things are coming at you from all directions. I am more aware of time when I feel pressured. There is almost this internal clock within your head, where you can hear the ticking. (Christine)

The fact that too much time and too little time are both stressful suggests that the problem lies in the very measurement of time, the ticking of your internal clock. A solution is to replace the counting of time with a sense of the rhythms and routines of daily life and work. If time is the rhythm of life, it doesn't need to be managed and struggled against: you're not forced to blame yourself for your inability to adhere to a rigid timetable.

Time-budgets never work unless they become a rhythm of life.

How timetables work

The nice thing about a wholistic approach to time organisation is that it is simple. You don't have to devise a complicated system. Probably the simpler, the better.

The basic element of any time plan is a timetable. This is an externalised, spatial arrangement of weekly activities that are separated and given a specific place and time. This helps prevent that overwhelming feeling of things collapsing upon each other. You don't have to hold 'all the things you have to do' in your head because it's out there, on the table. Here are some of the things that you'll want to include:

- formal class times: tutorials and lectures;
- your own daily study times: reading, writing and class preparation;
- regular recreational activities you engage in: sport, walking, music and so on;
- paid employment.

Remember that the purpose of your timetable is to alleviate pressure, not to create a test of your work ethic. Ensure that you do not fill in the whole of your week, for you will leave yourself feeling blocked rather than spacious.

It is through producing this sense of space that timetables facilitate learning. Let's explain how.

- Timetables allow you to attend to what's at hand. For example, when you have a timetabled class, *that* is where you have to be at that time. This obligation permits you to leave your worries about yesterday or tomorrow at the door. Three hours of class time become time-out. And since you're really present in the class, you can engage fully in the learning process. The same principle can be used if you set particular regular times for reading, working on essay drafts or writing in a journal.

- Timetables can make work easy. For example, if you set an hour a day for writing in your journal, you do not have to wait for the right time, for spare time, for a good thought to come along. You become less judgmental about what you write because your obligation is simply to write. This is what Vicky says about such rituals:

  I had to discipline myself to sit down at my desk to write in a workbook. This action is creating a controlled atmosphere where I am forcing myself to write. However, after I make the initial step I change my perception to thinking 'Well, I'm here writing now so I may as well put all my energy into it'. This in turn allows me to be creative in this controlled atmosphere. When I wrote the first entry of this workbook I was meeting a friend in about an hour. Now I am a person usually very conscious of the time but when I was focused in this book I couldn't believe that I was now half an hour late for my friend! (Vicky)

- Some of your most important thinking, your insights and flashes, will come unbidden, in time that is beyond timetables, in the shower, on the beach or on the bus. By taking care of those formal things that have to be attended to, a timetable can give us time for these informal learning experiences.
- A timetable gives the rest that is essential for creative work.

  A timetable is a great tool in times of stress ... If I'm not working to a timetable during study time, I can't let myself relax enough to have breaks, therefore my work

> *is stilted and unresponsive due to hours and hours of continuous study. But when I'm timetabled, I can enjoy my breaks as I say to myself – you deserve this time-out! (Miranda)*

- If you're busy juggling study, domestic responsibilities and paid employment, you may start to wonder how you're ever going to make time for all your commitments. Timetables can help by raising the question that begs to be asked: *can* everything be done? Be honest with yourself. If you're overcommitted, it is best to face this early. You will need to decide if something has to be jettisoned: a few weeks' income? the quality of your study? one of your subjects? your Saturday nights? Students who face this choice return to their work with a sense of relief: *something has to go, and for now it will be* … . Those who stay in denial want to do everything at every moment but do nothing with care or respect.
- The problem of deadlines doesn't arise for students who adopt a step-by-step approach to writing. By timetabling specific tasks, week-by-week, they can attend to what's at hand and trust the process to carry them along. Rather than the daunting sense of an essay or report or research project to be completed, there is just this task to perform this week, each week, this number of words to be done. An essay will emerge through the process, without panic, without the usual worries about deadlines.

Timetables can alleviate the pressure of the internal clock.

Structure and freedom

When students say they cannot work without the pressure of deadlines, what they really want are supportive structures. Listen to Vicky:

> *During my holidays I had half the weekdays to myself as my boyfriend had to work. I was so bored, I craved uni work. I craved knowledge, something structured that someone else could tell me what to do. However, I felt too, that if I did have any pressing uni work I had to do I'd just be avoiding it like the plague. As it turned out I did fill this nothingness with walking, a routine that I frequently practised before I moved to Sydney. I started also to draw and without realising it started to think about where I was at in life. (Vicky)*

Instead of waiting for someone else to fix her boredom, Vicky herself provided the structure she felt she needed. Falling into the rhythms of her routines, she felt safe and open at the same time, no longer wasting time and nervous energy making ad hoc decisions.

Remember, though, that the aim of timetables is to ease pressures and anxieties, not to create a new set. Don't get obsessed with time management. Your timetable should lighten the pressure of the clock in your head. If you can forget clock time, it's working well. As Vicky says of her journal routines:

> *This ritual allowed my creativity to flourish and time to lapse. So much so that it wasn't uncommon for me to look up above my page of writing to see the clock say 12.30. (Vicky)*

A timetable provides a structure to facilitate freedom and fluency. It should be used flexibly and not become a constraint. So if you are absorbed in a conversation with friends, or if you are lost in your thoughts while out on a walk, or if, like Vicky, you are in a flow of writing, do not stop because of what the clock says. The timetable is designed to encourage just such experiences.

Timetables can give you creative freedom.

TAKING IT EASY

Health

> *I go through stages with my health: the 'don't care' stage where business overwhelms me and I don't exercise or watch my food. Or the 'health conscious' stage, where I exercise a few times a week and eat healthy. At the moment I'm going through an in-between stage ... I'm trying to get healthy again but am finding it difficult to kick the junk food/lazy habits. (Michelle)*

Michelle assumes that while it is easy to be unhealthy, health is an achievement that comes from hard work and self-sacrifice. But life need not feel so torn between indulgence and duty. As Miranda suggests, you can take care of yourself by taking it easy:

> *'Wholistic' is a favourite word of mine at the moment. I think it should be the way we view our lives – not to split it up into a 'uni' pigeonhole, 'work' pigeonhole and so on, but to take a moment to step back and to look at our lives like somebody meeting us for the first time. It is almost that the more students push themselves – work more, study more, write more, party more – the more we are seen as succeeding at uni ... Taking care doesn't necessarily mean cutting down, as I have found some of my most productive months have been when I have had a*

> *very full schedule, both work-related and extra-curricular ... In my life, it has been that looking long-term puts myself into perspective, how well I'm looking after myself, my mental, physical and emotional health, too! After all, you won't live long enough to enjoy your long-distance plan if you aren't healthy in mind, body and spirit. (Miranda)*

Miranda reminds us that we make things hard for ourselves when we assume that struggle gives experiences their value. *Am I working hard enough? Do I deserve any time off? Can I afford the time to go for a swim, go for a walk, restock the fridge?* But when work and life aren't competing, they can support each other. There is, as Miranda implies, a connection between health and whole: rather than being a separate compartment, health *means* the connection of different parts of life.

This wholistic view doesn't pose health as the simple elimination of pain or difficulty. It doesn't deny the pressures of everyday life, or suggest that you can run away from difficult times. It proposes that health arises from the way you meet whatever circumstances you are presented with. It means, for example, not giving yourself a hard time about hard times – *Why can't I cope better? Why can't I solve this problem? Is it my fault?* It means being able to say 'it's okay not to feel okay'. It means treating yourself as compassionately as you'd treat others.

Health is the connection between different parts of life.

Recreation

In busy everyday life, how do we, as Miranda put it, take a moment to meet the world and ourselves as if for the first time? Rachel gives a clue:

> *I often find intense feelings of gratitude and wonder only usually occur in the holidays when I'm relaxed. During the term or when I'm at work I find I'm too tired or stressed to let go and see things differently. I'm usually too focused on long hours and deadlines to experience gratitude and wonder and beauty of the world. It's sad really, because the world is such an amazing place when one sees things differently, and is in-relation with them.*
>
> *Inspiration, breathing, beauty, wonder, it's all around me everyday and in order to experience it all you need is to be with them. However, knowing this I still find myself tied up in the stress of everyday life trying to fit in as many activities as possible on as little sleep as possible. I find it very hard to let go! Most days are about hanging in there instead of fully living.*
>
> *Perhaps it's a process that requires a lot of practice. I have on many occasions been completely inspired as I lie on the sandy beaches in summer. I don't know if it's just me, but unless I'm relaxing on holidays, this feeling rarely comes to me. It's sad really. (Rachel)*

Rachel talks of a life divided between the stress of work on the one hand and holiday relaxation on the other, but she recognises that this split only exists when she cannot 'let go'. If recreation is understood to be part of life's rhythms, it becomes an everyday source of energy. Every day can be a holiday: you don't need to wait for vacations to play netball, lie on a beach or go for a walk. And you can be sure that, as part of a healthy life, such recreations will benefit your university work.

Let's see how this benefit arises. Joyce gives the example of walking:

> *For me these moments of clarity and inspiration come when I am unsuspecting and sort of jump out at me, surprising me. Trying to force them just seems to push them away. These moments are serene moments of stillness, where your mind is calm and focused, these brief seconds of understanding, however, are often followed by a stampede of continuous thoughts and questions racing through your mind.*
>
> *I must admit that when I am outside walking at a continuous and steady pace I have the majority of these moments, but is it really the isolation, fresh air, the idea of moving forward and the rhythm of the walking that is helping these moments enter my mind? Or am I already in the mental state needed to arouse these thoughts before I decided to go for a walk? (Joyce)*

The answer to Joyce's question is 'probably both'. Think about how walking feels: to start with, the walk might seem difficult; you are aware of your effort, of moving your legs, of the distance you have to travel. And then you find that something has shifted. Tiredness, aches, difficulty have disappeared. The rhythm of walking is carrying you. It now feels effortless because it is no longer *you* who is doing the walking. Things enter your mind without your effort. Thoughts become clear and you now know what it is you were previously unable to say.

Writers often speak of the miraculous effects of movement. Dante is famous for the pairs of shoes he wore out in the process of writing. When blocked or stuck – in your writing and thinking, emotionally or physically – movement easily gets you back into the flow of things.

In everyday recreation there is creation.

Safe places

If there are recreational activities that allow inspiration, there are also particular places. Lucy tells us how these places work:

> *I think the reason why we have such brilliant ideas in the odd Eureka places, showering, cleaning, exercising, gardening is because we are no longer watching ourselves. The mental block of the sheer fact that you are trying so hard to watch your self trying prevents you achieving. People ask, 'how did you come up with that?' or 'where did that idea come from?'. I can't answer, I know that it came from within me but I didn't exactly have a logic, step by step thought pattern that culminated in the idea. At times it just comes to you from inside and outside, from me and my mind and the ethereal outside forces. It's not like thinking, oh this leads to this which leads to that and finally Eureka! No. It just pops into your head. (Lucy)*

Feeling whole only occurs in spaces where you do not have to watch yourself. 'A room of one's own' is Virginia Woolf's famous phrase for these spaces. This doesn't imply that students need to withdraw from the world of everyday relations. On the contrary, rooms of our own give us the protection we need in order to be open to the world. These are places where we can *hang out*, where we can accept the ideas that come to us.

A safe space doesn't have to be a room. It might be a daily routine or your journal, for instance, or the shower, or a corner in the house or, as in Rachel's case, in the garden:

> *See, in my garden I have a small patch out the front – it's 'my patch', my little piece of earth. Beside my vegie patch is a giant mulberry tree. It's been out the front much longer than we've lived in the house, like an inter-generational heirloom, grounded in the garden.*
>
> *The reason I mention the mulberry tree is it's currently in season. Thousands of black mulberries hide between the branches of the old tree, providing a delicious natural buffet for an array of animals including bats, possums, and many birds.*
>
> *I've noticed a pair of birds in the mulberry tree once that totally blew me away. I had never seen anything like them before. They must be incredibly rare, because I've never heard of any bird that resembles them, and I've been searching on the internet and bird encyclopedias for a while.*
>
> *These birds are large, grey birds with a flared tail that looks just like a kookaburra's, only they have incredibly long narrow necks and small heads with a beak that looks*

rounded and quite wide. Their heads almost look like sea gulls I suppose, only with wide beaks, and much larger than a sea gull.

The most amazing thing about them is the noise they make. It's a low rumbly screak that sounds just like a kookaburra, only lower. And you can hear their call so far away! I was so amazed when I first saw them. I raced inside to get a camera but they had flown away. Perhaps they come from an area very far away ...

The reason I mentioned all this is because these observations all occur when I'm watering my vegie patch. We have a rather long driveway, and I rarely walk up it. Usually I drive straight past the mulberry tree without even noticing whether or not the fruit had even developed or not. Since I established my vegie patch, I'm spending more time outside and I'm able to enjoy the natural beauty that surrounds me.

As you can see, my vegie patch is a source of therapy. It is my way of letting go from the stress of everyday life. It's an excuse to go outside and enjoy the sunshine and fresh air. I get a sense of achievement and purpose out of watering my vegie patch, as the seedlings are relying on the water I provide them in order to survive. (Rachel)

Rachel's garden gives her recreation everyday. It is a safe place that allows her to rediscover her sense of vitality and interest. Without effort, she has a sense of wholeness that lets her know what is most important in life.

Cherish the places where you do not need to watch yourself. In these places you will discover what matters most to you.

Making choices

Every day at university you will be making choices, ranging from major decisions about what courses to study to small decisions about what essay to write. The ability to make effective choices is one of the skills that university teaches. Choices are a *part of* and not just a *means to* your education.

Lucy's and Rachel's accounts above can help us understand the processes that allow good choices. Both emphasised the need for safe places. And in Vicky's case, this safety was provided by a jetty:

> *I get revelations in many weird places. One major revelation that I had last term occurred when I was sitting on a jetty looking over the harbour. Though this sounds picturesque, what took my attention was little bits of wood on the jetty which I pulled off and threw into the water. As I was doing this, a problem which I had faced all term suddenly fixed itself. The problem was deciding what course I was going to try and transfer into next year. I had always wanted to do a psychology degree all through my final years of high school, but moving to*

Sydney before last term, and living with my cousin and his girlfriend, who were both lawyers, suddenly made me feel that psych wasn't good enough. I didn't want to pigeonhole myself into a psych course and then realise I would have done much better doing something else.

So I went on the hunt, looking at Arts/Law, Arts/ Commerce and got more frustrated as the term went on. My motivation to do my work in any of my term 1 subjects waned too, because I felt I had nothing to aspire to. What was I going to do? I felt so lost, and after a whole term and a whole holidays trying I was going to move to Newcastle University.

But then after basically making the decision to move, I went to the jetty and relaxed. That's when it came to me that psych and not commerce or law was my calling. That it wasn't easy to get into psych because of its popularity but that didn't mean it was not for me and that I wasn't unique. I couldn't believe it: after all that semester of trying to plan, to decide, the one moment I forgot about the problem was the moment the problem and confusion sailed away. (Vicky)

Vicky makes a valuable distinction between decisions and callings. Good choices rely on appreciation of the aspects of life not ordered through decisions. Decisions are hard to make, and to stick to. We want this career. But we also want that career, it's really cool. And then a week later we can't resist this better job that our friend has discovered. We want everything. Callings, on the other hand, come as a still sense of clarity. They tell us where we belong.

If you listen to your heart when making choices, you won't fall into the common trap of doing things for reasons of fear or status or rewards. You will be doing what you love, so the work process itself becomes easy and enriching. You will be doing what you do best.

Do what you love doing.

So what matters most at university? This is Christine's conclusion:

> *There is so much to do, see and experience and so little time. This often results in hectic schedules and running from one thing to another. This to many people seems like a lively, intense lifestyle. However, you can achieve this same liveliness and vitality in a very different way – by treating your life as a gift to be cherished, appreciated and made use of.*
>
> *Vitality is a feeling not achieved by consuming yourself in many, varied fast paced tasks, but from getting joy from doing something. To feel passionate about what you are doing and immersing yourself in that moment and really experiencing and appreciating something brings about a feeling of liveliness and intensity.*
>
> *It is almost what you make of your life with what you are given that counts. To take care of yourself does not have to involve indulging yourself in luxuries. It is to be thankful for who and what you are, to be aware of the gift of life. To take care is to respect yourself, both in a physical and emotional sense. (Christine)*

FURTHER READING

The ideas underlying this book are more fully spelled out in two of our earlier books: *The Mystery of Everyday Life* (The Federation Press, Sydney, 2002), which concentrates on the themes of participation and wholeness, and *Passionate Sociology* (Sage, London, 1996), which analyses the social relations of university work at greater length.

Some books which influenced us are:

G Bachelard: *The Poetics of Space* (Beacon, Boston, 1969)
M Buber: *I and Thou* (Scribner's, New York, 1958)
D Bohm and FD Peat: *Science, Order and Creativity* (Bantam, Toronto, 1987)
M Epstein: *Thoughts Without A Thinker* (Basic Books, New York, 1995)
M Merleau-Ponty: *The Visible and the Invisible* (Northwestern University Press, Evanston, 1968)
M Serres: *Angels: A Modern Myth* (Flammarion, Paris, 1995)

Journal Notes

Journal Notes

Journal Notes

Journal Notes

Journal Notes

Journal Notes

Journal Notes

Journal Notes

Journal Notes